ELMHURST PUBLIC LIBRARY

3 1135 00992 04█

P9-CDC-811

THE
CIVIL WAR
A NATION DIVIDED

Civil War
Leaders

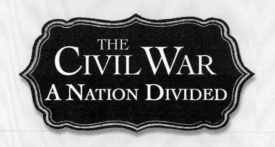

THE CIVIL WAR
A NATION DIVIDED

J
973.7092
MCN

THE CIVIL WAR
A NATION DIVIDED

Civil War
Leaders

Tim McNeese

ELMHURST PUBLIC LIBRARY
125 S. PROSPECT AVE.
ELMHURST, IL 60126

CHELSEA HOUSE
PUBLISHERS
An imprint of Infobase Publishing

CIVIL WAR LEADERS

Copyright © 2009 by Infobase Publishing

All rights reserved. No part of this book may be reproduced or utilized in any form or by any means, electronic or mechanical, including photocopying, recording, or by any information storage or retrieval systems, without permission in writing from the publisher. For information, contact:

Chelsea House
An imprint of Infobase Publishing
132 West 31st Street
New York NY 10001

Library of Congress Cataloging-in-Publication Data
McNeese, Tim.
  Civil War leaders / Tim McNeese.
    p. cm. — (Civil War, a nation divided)
  Includes bibliographical references and index.
  ISBN 978-1-60413-033-1 (hardcover)
  1. United States—History—Civil War, 1861–1865—Biography—Juvenile literature. 2. Leadership—History—19th century—Juvenile literature. I. Title. II. Series.

  E467.M436 2009
  973.70922—dc22   2009000655

Chelsea House books are available at special discounts when purchased in bulk quantities for businesses, associations, institutions, or sales promotions. Please call our Special Sales Department in New York at (212) 967-8800 or (800) 322-8755.

You can find Chelsea House on the World Wide Web at
http://www.chelseahouse.com

Series design by Lina Farinella
Cover design by Takeshi Takahashi

Printed in the United States of America

Bang NMSG 10 9 8 7 6 5 4 3 2 1

This book is printed on acid-free paper.

All links and Web addresses were checked and verified to be correct at the time of publication. Because of the dynamic nature of the Web, some addresses and links may have changed since publication and may no longer be valid.

Contents

Chronology

1820   The Missouri Compromise allows Maine to be admitted to the Union as a free state and Missouri as a slave state in 1821.

1831   William Lloyd Garrison publishes the first issue of his abolitionist newspaper, *The Liberator*.

1836   The House of Representatives passes a gag rule that automatically tables or postpones action on all petitions relating to slavery without hearing them.

1838   The Underground Railroad is formally organized.

1845   Former slave Frederick Douglass publishes his autobiography, *Narrative of the Life of Frederick Douglass, An American Slave*.

1850   Congress enacts several measures that together make up the Compromise of 1850.

1852   Harriet Beecher Stowe publishes *Uncle Tom's Cabin*.

1854   Congress passes the Kansas-Nebraska Act, which overturns the Missouri Compromise and thus opens Northern territories to slavery.

1855   As Kansas prepares to vote, thousands of Border Ruffians from Missouri enter the territory in an attempt to influence the elections. This begins the period known as Bleeding Kansas.

1856   South Carolina representative Preston Brooks attacks Massachusetts senator Charles Sumner on the Senate floor and beats him with a cane.

1857   The Supreme Court rules, in *Dred Scott v. Sandford,* that blacks are not U.S. citizens and slaveholders have the right to take slaves into free areas of the country.

1859   John Brown seizes the arsenal at Harpers Ferry, Virginia. Robert E. Lee, then a Federal Army regular, leads the troops that capture Brown.

1860   **NOVEMBER**   Abraham Lincoln is elected president.

        DECEMBER   A South Carolina convention passes an ordinance of secession, and the state secedes from the Union.

1861   **JANUARY**   Florida, Alabama, Georgia, and Louisiana secede from the Union.

        FEBRUARY   Texas votes to secede from the Union. The Confederate States of America is formed and elects Jefferson Davis as its president.

        MARCH   Abraham Lincoln is sworn in as the sixteenth president of the United States and delivers his first inaugural address.

        APRIL 12   At 4:30 A.M., Confederate forces fire on South Carolina's Fort Sumter. The Civil War begins. Virginia secedes from the Union five days later.

        MAY   Arkansas and North Carolina secede from the Union.

        JUNE   Tennessee secedes from the Union.

        JULY 21   The Union suffers a defeat in northern Virginia, at the First Battle of Bull Run (Manassas).

        AUGUST   The Confederates win the Battle of Wilson's Creek, in Missouri.

1862   **FEBRUARY 6**   In Tennessee, Union general Ulysses S. Grant captures Fort Henry. Ten days later, he captures Fort Donelson.

MARCH The Confederate ironclad ship CSS *Virginia* (formerly the USS *Merrimack*) battles the Union ironclad *Monitor* to a draw. The Union's Peninsular Campaign begins in Virginia.

APRIL 6–7 Ulysses S. Grant defeats Confederate forces in the Battle of Shiloh (Pittsburg Landing), in Tennessee.

APRIL 24 David Farragut moves his fleet of Union Navy vessels up the Mississippi River to take New Orleans.

MAY 31 The Battle of Seven Pines (Fair Oaks) takes place in Virginia.

JUNE 1 Robert E. Lee assumes command of the Army of Northern Virginia.

JUNE 25–JULY 1 The Seven Days Battles are fought in Virginia.

AUGUST 29–30 The Union is defeated at the Second Battle of Bull Run.

SEPTEMBER 17 The bloodiest day in U.S. military history: Confederate forces under Robert E. Lee are stopped at Antietam, Maryland, by Union forces under George B. McClellan.

SEPTEMBER 22 The first Emancipation Proclamation to free slaves in the rebellious states is issued by President Lincoln.

DECEMBER 13 The Union's Army of the Potomac, under Ambrose Burnside, suffers a costly defeat at Fredericksburg, Virginia.

1863 **JANUARY 1** President Lincoln issues the final Emancipation Proclamation.

JANUARY 29 Ulysses S. Grant is placed in command of the Army of the West, with orders to capture Vicksburg, Mississippi.

MAY 1–4   Union forces under Joseph Hooker are defeated decisively by Robert E. Lee's much smaller forces at the Battle of Chancellorsville, in Virginia.

MAY 10   The South suffers a huge blow as General Thomas "Stonewall" Jackson dies from wounds he received during the battle of Chancellorsville.

JUNE 3   Robert E. Lee launches his second invasion of the North; he heads into Pennsylvania with 75,000 Confederate troops.

JULY 1–3   The tide of war turns against the South as the Confederates are defeated at the Battle of Gettysburg in Pennsylvania.

JULY 4   Vicksburg, the last Confederate stronghold on the Mississippi River, surrenders to Ulysses S. Grant after a six-week siege.

JULY 13–16   Antidraft riots rip through New York City.

JULY 18   The black 54th Massachusetts Infantry Regiment under Colonel Robert Gould Shaw assaults a fortified Confederate position at Fort Wagner, South Carolina.

SEPTEMBER 19–20   A decisive Confederate victory takes place at Chickamauga, Tennessee.

NOVEMBER 19   President Lincoln delivers the Gettysburg Address.

NOVEMBER 23–25   Ulysses S. Grant's Union forces win an important victory at the Battle of Chattanooga, in Tennessee.

1864   **MARCH 9**   President Lincoln names Ulysses S. Grant general-in-chief of all the armies of the United States.

MAY 4   Ulysses S. Grant opens a massive, coordinated campaign against Robert E. Lee's Confederate armies in Virginia.

MAY 5–6 The Battle of the Wilderness is fought in Virginia.

MAY 8–12 The Battle of Spotsylvania is fought in Virginia.

JUNE 1–3 The Battle of Cold Harbor is fought in Virginia.

JUNE 15 Union forces miss an opportunity to capture Petersburg, Virginia; this results in a nine-month Union siege of the city.

SEPTEMBER 2 Atlanta, Georgia, is captured by Union forces led by William Tecumseh Sherman.

OCTOBER 19 Union general Philip H. Sheridan wins a decisive victory over Confederate general Jubal Early in the Shenandoah Valley of Virginia.

NOVEMBER 8 Abraham Lincoln is reelected president, defeating Democratic challenger George B. McClellan.

NOVEMBER 15 General William T. Sherman begins his March to the Sea from Atlanta.

DECEMBER 15–16 Confederate general John Bell Hood is defeated at Nashville, Tennessee, by Union forces under George H. Thomas.

DECEMBER 21 General Sherman reaches Savannah, Georgia; he leaves behind a path of destruction 300 miles long and 60 miles wide from Atlanta to the sea.

1865 Southern states begin to pass Black Codes.

JANUARY 31 The U.S. Congress approves the Thirteenth Amendment to the United States Constitution.

FEBRUARY 3 A peace conference takes place as President Lincoln meets with Confederate vice president Alexander Stephens at Hampton Roads, Virginia; the meeting ends in failure, and the war continues.

MARCH 4 Lincoln delivers his second inaugural address ("With Malice Toward None"). Congress establishes the Freedmen's Bureau.

MARCH 25   Robert E. Lee's Army of Northern Virginia begins its last offensive with an attack on the center of Ulysses S. Grant's forces at Petersburg, Virginia. Four hours later, Lee's attack is broken.

APRIL 2   Grant's forces begin a general advance and break through Lee's lines at Petersburg. Lee evacuates Petersburg. Richmond, Virginia, the Confederate capital, is evacuated.

APRIL 9   Robert E. Lee surrenders his Confederate Army to Ulysses S. Grant at the village of Appomattox Court House, Virginia.

APRIL 14   John Wilkes Booth shoots President Lincoln at Ford's Theatre in Washington, D.C.

APRIL 15   President Abraham Lincoln dies. Vice President Andrew Johnson assumes the presidency.

APRIL 18   Confederate general Joseph E. Johnston surrenders to Union general William T. Sherman in North Carolina.

APRIL 26   John Wilkes Booth is shot and killed in a tobacco barn in Virginia.

DECEMBER   The Thirteenth Amendment is ratified.

1866   Congress approves the Fourteenth Amendment to the Constitution.

Congress passes the Civil Rights Act.

The responsibilities and powers of the Freedmen's Bureau are expanded by Congress. The legislation is vetoed by President Johnson, but Congress overrides his veto.

The Ku Klux Klan is established in Tennessee.

1867   Congress passes the Military Reconstruction Act.

Congress passes the Tenure of Office Act.

1868   The impeachment trial of President Andrew Johnson ends in acquittal.

Ulysses S. Grant is elected president.

1869   Congress approves the Fifteenth Amendment to the Constitution.

1871   The Ku Klux Klan Act is passed by Congress.

1872   President Grant is reelected.

1875   A new Civil Rights Act is passed.

1877   Rutherford B. Hayes assumes the presidency. The Reconstruction Era ends.

Abraham Lincoln

It would prove to be the bloodiest war in U.S. history and one of the most dividing. In all, the Civil War was responsible for the deaths of 620,000 American combatants, largely from wounds and disease. The breakdown for each side reveals about 360,000 Union and 260,000 Confederates killed. This staggering number barely falls short of the 680,000 Americans who died in all other U.S. wars combined! In 1861, when the Civil War opened, the nation was home to 30 million people, including 7 million slaves. Nearly every American living during the war knew someone who died in the conflict. Mothers and fathers lost sons, wives never saw their husbands return home, children were forced to grow up fatherless, and siblings mourned their departed brothers. The experience of the Civil War deeply changed the country. Personal responses are found in the letters, diaries, and other sources that have survived during nearly a century and a half since the war.

Hundreds of thousands of lives were lost and millions of lives were altered by the four-year-long national struggle.

Most of those names are forgotten or lost in the mists of time. History best remembers the names of several key individuals whose actions and contributions during the war helped to shape the course of the conflict itself, and even the direction of the United States after the war was over. Their contributions took place on the battlefield, in the halls of legislative power, and in the offices of executive leadership. This book will present the lives and contributions made by six such individuals, representatives of both sides in the conflict, Northerners and Southerners alike.

Leading up to the war, the United States became increasingly fractured and turned to secession and battle when all other alternatives seemed lost. The nation emerged on the other side of the conflict united, its weaknesses healed, and its future more secure than it had been before the war had ruled the country's landscape. The efforts during this war of the six leaders in this book may, at times, have pitted one against the other. When taken together, their legacies represent a patchwork quilt of American biographies.

THE MAN FROM ILLINOIS

Perhaps no man faced greater challenges as president or had a greater impact on the legacy of the Civil War than did Abraham Lincoln. Today, he is seen as one of the greatest presidents of the United States, but this honor was won at great personal cost. The controversies that had raged across the nineteenth-century republic, with its regional divisions and disagreements over slavery, finally came to a head in the early 1860s. This led the nation into war, just as Lincoln was preparing to take office as the nation's sixteenth chief executive. Four years of bloody war divided the nation and marred his presidency from its beginning. Yet in the end, Lincoln managed to restore the whole of the fractured Union and witnessed the return of the Confederate states into a new and morally stronger nation.

His country, as himself, had been tested by fire. Together, both prevailed. During the long nightmare of the war, he, along with the U.S. Congress, addressed the ultimate extinction of slavery in the United States. During the summer of 1862, he penned the Emancipation Proclamation, which began the political processes of eliminating slavery from the country's landscape. Through his courageous and sometimes controversial decision making, the United States and its people not only weathered the combined challenges represented by secession, division, and civil war, but emerged, in the words of Lincoln's famous Gettysburg Address, with "a new birth of freedom." Truly, Lincoln stands tall as one of the greatest of American leaders.

FRONTIER YOUTH

Abraham Lincoln was born in a one-room log cabin in Larue County (then southeast Hardin County), Kentucky, on February 12, 1809. His parents, Thomas Lincoln and Nancy Hanks, were undereducated pioneers. An earlier Lincoln ancestor, Samuel Lincoln, had come to the United States during the 1600s, arriving at Hingham, Massachusetts. Through the years, the other Lincolns had moved from the Atlantic seaboard inward, toward the frontier to Pennsylvania, Virginia, and across the Appalachian Mountains. At the time of Abraham's birth, his father was an upstanding leader in the Kentucky backwoods, where he had purchased his land, Sinking Spring Farm, just a few months earlier. The Lincolns were members of a Hard-shell Baptist church, a common faith among the country's early-nineteenth-century pioneers. In his adult years, Abraham Lincoln never officially joined the church of his parents, nor did he become an official member of any other Christian faith tradition.

His family moved 10 miles (16 kilometers) away from its rough frontier residence two years later. In 1816, Thomas Lincoln decided to move his family to Indiana. Life was hard there, for Indiana was still frontier backcountry. The Lincolns spent their first winter in what was called a half-faced camp, a three-sided lean-to cabin made of split logs. They were constantly exposed to the winter weather and kept a campfire going at all times on the open side of their cabin. This kept wild animals away and provided some warmth. Although he was young, Abraham was expected to work hard, complete chores, and help on the farm. By age eight, he was big enough to wield an ax.

The family was struck with tragedy when Abraham's mother, Nancy, died in 1818. The Lincolns continued on without her, and the next year Thomas Lincoln married a woman from Kentucky, Sarah Bush Johnston. She brought with her three children from an earlier marriage and helped fill the Lincoln home with happiness. She and young Abraham shared a special bond and were extremely close. Ironically, Abraham and his father remained distant during all of the future president's life. They were so estranged that, when his father died, the adult Lincoln did not even attend the funeral. Later in life, he said of his stepmother, according to historian David Donald, "All that I am or ever hope to be I owe to her."

Through these wilderness years, young Abraham grew into manhood. During his youth, he attended school infrequently. Historians estimate that he might have attended a total of 18 months of school. He did learn to read, even if he was largely self-taught. Abraham loved books and borrowed them wherever and from whomever he could. He became a rugged frontier lad, eventually reaching a height of 6 feet 4 inches (1.9 meters). He was strong, and he even engaged in local wrestling matches with other boys. When Abraham was 11, his family moved to Perry County (today's Spencer County), Indiana. Thomas Lincoln may have been forced to make the move. Often, pioneer land claims were unofficial and legal papers were rare. He may have had difficulty proving he had legal title to his farm in Hardin County. In 1830, when Abraham Lincoln turned 21, his father moved the family again, to public land in Macon County, Illinois.

Abraham Lincoln's childhood home (above) was a primitive cabin in Indiana. Born without many privileges and opportunities, Lincoln spent much of his young life working on the family farm instead of going to school. Despite his lack of education, the future president loved to read and would walk for miles just to borrow a book.

WAR AND POLITICS

By age 22, Abraham Lincoln left home and hired himself out to a trader to help take a flatboat down the Ohio and Mississippi rivers to New Orleans. The trader later hired Lincoln to work in his general store in the village of New Salem, Illinois. Illinois remained Lincoln's home for the next 30 years.

The several years following his arrival in New Salem were formative for young Lincoln. His work as a store clerk brought little income, but he spent much of his time borrowing books and reading the classics. In 1832, he became involved in a frontier Indian conflict that would be remembered as the Black Hawk War. He was popular among his fellow Illinois volunteers and was elected captain of the militia company whose ranks were filled with men and boys from New Salem. According to historian Roy Basler, the future president later wrote that he had never had "any such success in life which gave him so much satisfaction" as his appointment as captain. He and his militia unit saw no action during the short-lived conflict.

A year after the Black Hawk War, Lincoln was appointed postmaster of New Salem. Later, he worked as a surveyor. In 1834, he ran in his first political race for the state legislature and won. He served four terms as a member of the Whig Party, which had been established only recently as an alternative to President Andrew Jackson's Democratic Party. Through these years, Lincoln studied law and was admitted to the bar in 1837. At that time, he moved from the small settlement of New Salem to Springfield, where he would live until he left Illinois for the last time to become president. For the next several years, Lincoln shared a practice with several different partners. He then served four consecutive terms in the Illinois House of Representatives, representing Sangamon County.

This was only the beginning of Lincoln's long political career. In 1846, Lincoln ran for the U.S. House of Representatives as a Whig and again won. During Lincoln's single term as a U.S. representative, the United States entered the Mexican-American War. President James K. Polk, from Tennessee, had pushed the Mexicans into the conflict through a controversy over the southwestern boundary of the new state of Texas, a former Mexican province. Although Lincoln was only a freshman representative, he spoke out with his concerns and disapproval of the war. He claimed the Democrat Polk had entered the war for his own glory, and he even challenged Polk's assertion that he had taken the U.S. military into the war after American soldiers had been killed on "American soil." Lincoln offered what were called the "spot" resolutions, demanding that Polk show exactly the "spot" where American blood had been shed. On other occasions, too, Lincoln spoke out against Polk and the Democrats over the war. Prior to the next election year, the Democrats campaigned heavily in Illinois, especially in Lincoln's district. The Mexican-American War had been popular there, with several locals having served as volunteers during the conflict. Lincoln's words against the war became controversial, and he chose not to run for reelection.

After leaving the national legislature, Lincoln returned to law. By the late 1840s and early 1850s, he was a well-established, well-known lawyer in Illinois and was becoming prosperous. In the courtroom, he was known for his hard and direct cross-examinations and for his solid closing arguments. For many years, he partnered with William Herndon, a fellow Whig, and the two men shared law offices. In retirement, after Lincoln's death, Herndon wrote down as many stories about Lincoln as he could recall, publishing them in the book *Herndon's Lincoln*.

In 1842, Lincoln married Mary Todd, a woman 10 years younger than himself. She was from Kentucky, where her father was a prominent plantation and slave owner. The Lincolns were married for 23 years until Abraham's death, and they had four children, all boys. Mary became pregnant shortly after their wedding, giving birth to Robert Lincoln on August 1, 1843. A second child, Edward Baker Lincoln, came along three years later and died at age four in 1850. Their third boy, William "Willie" Wallace Lincoln, was born later the same year and died during Lincoln's presidency. Their youngest, Thomas "Tad" Lincoln, was born in 1853 and died at age 18. Only Robert would survive into adulthood. The deaths of their boys weighed heavily on the Lincolns. Mary became unstable in later years, to the point where her son Robert committed her to a sanitarium.

A DIVIDING NATION

By 1854, Lincoln was drawn back into politics. The country was already showing the signs of division over the issue of expanding slavery into the nation's western territories. Lincoln was inspired to get back into politics by the proposed Kansas-Nebraska bill, which was introduced in Congress by Illinois senator Stephen Douglas. The bill would, at least in theory, allow slavery in a non-slave territory. Lincoln did not approve of the bill and was led to campaign on behalf of candidates who were also opposed to the proposed law.

To Douglas, the Kansas-Nebraska bill, which would authorize a political theory called popular sovereignty, made great sense. Popular sovereignty, to Douglas, was democracy in action, since it would give the people of a territory the right to vote on whether they wanted slavery in their territory or not, rather than having Congress determine the issue for them.

Lincoln saw things differently, as revealed in his Peoria Speech, which he delivered on October 16, 1854:

> [The act has a] declared indifference, but as I must think, covert real zeal for the spread of slavery, I cannot but hate it. I hate it because of the monstrous injustice of slavery itself. I hate it because it deprives our republican example of its just influence in the world—enables the enemies of free institutions, with plausibility, to taunt us as hypocrites—causes the real friends of freedom to doubt our sincerity, and especially because it forces so many really good men amongst ourselves into an open war with the very fundamental principles of civil liberty—criticizing the Declaration of Independence, and insisting that there is no right principle of action but self-interest.

Despite such speech from Lincoln and other opponents, the Kansas-Nebraska bill became law as the Kansas-Nebraska Act. This led to a shake-up in the U.S. political party system. The

Above, *Abraham and Mary Todd Lincoln are pictured with their sons Willie, Tad, and Robert. Tad and Willie Lincoln were rowdy, mischievous boys who often interrupted their father's meetings and caused chaos in the White House. Lincoln rarely disciplined his sons, preferring to use their youthful energy as an escape from the more pressing matters of the Civil War. Robert Lincoln, the eldest, was the only son of the president's to live past the age of 18.*

old Whig Party was dying. Lincoln and others, including former Whigs, and members of antislavery parties, including the Free Soil Party and Liberty Party, established a new party called the Republican Party. Lincoln would play crucial roles in the early years of the Republican Party.

THE CHALLENGER

In 1858, Lincoln was prepared to run against Stephen Douglas himself for his Senate seat. Lincoln, of course, was a Republican candidate. Speaking after his nomination, Lincoln said of the future of slavery in the country, as noted by historian Geoffrey Ward: "A house divided against itself cannot stand. I believe this government cannot endure, permanently half slave and half free. . . . It will become all one thing, or all the other." He was not only addressing the realities of the Kansas-Nebraska Act, which had opened up slavery to several western territories, but a key Supreme Court decision of the previous year, *Dred Scott v. Sandford*. In *Dred Scott*, the majority of the highest court in the land had stated that no blacks in the United States had any legal rights that any white man needed to recognize. And, the Court continued, Congress did not have the right to limit where slavery existed, including "free states and territories."

Under the U.S. Constitution at that time, senators were not selected directly by the vote of the people, but rather by the members of the state legislature. Nevertheless, Lincoln and Douglas "ran" for their nominations, agreeing to engage in a series of debates. The seven debates took place from August to October 1858, each presented in a different town or village in Illinois. The focus of the debates was the extension of slavery into the territories. At times, the two politicians sparred tooth and nail. In one debate, Senator Douglas told the assembled audience, according to historian Roy Basler: "If you desire Negro citizenship . . . if you desire them to vote on an equality with yourselves . . . then support Mr. Lincoln and the Black Republican party, who are in favor of the citizenship of the negro." Douglas spoke these words at a time when most white Americans did not believe blacks were equal to whites and certainly did not believe they should be given citizenship or the right to vote. Lincoln answered Douglas's attack with the following:

> I am not, nor ever have been, in favor of bringing about in any way the social and political equality of the white and black races, that I am not nor ever have been in favor of making voters or jurors of Negroes, nor of qualifying them to hold office, nor to intermarry with white people; and I will say in addition to this that there is a physical difference between the white and black races which I believe

will forever forbid the two races living together on terms of social and political equality. And inasmuch as they cannot so live, while they do remain together there must be a position of superior and inferior, and I as much as any other man am in favor of having the superior position assigned to the white race.

Lincoln's feelings on racial equality are clearly stated in these words. He may have been opposed to slavery and its extension into the western territories, but he did not see the two races as equals. To Lincoln, the only acceptable alternative to slavery was to send blacks "back" to Africa. For many years during his political career, Lincoln favored a colonization policy, believing the two races could not live side by side. As for the election, state legislators selected the incumbent, Stephen Douglas.

Two years later, Douglas and Lincoln ran against one another once again, only this time it was for the U.S. presidency. Through the 1858 senatorial race, Lincoln had become well known across the country as a leading Republican figure. When the Republican convention was held in Chicago, Lincoln was nominated as the presidential candidate for the party, beating other leading contenders, such as William H. Seward and Salmon P. Chase. (After Lincoln's election, he placed both men in his cabinet.)

The party chose Lincoln, in part because he was a westerner whom many thought might appeal to those voting in the new western territories and states. Also, Lincoln's political involvement so far had not gathered him many enemies. During the campaign, as well as throughout the 1850s, Lincoln claimed there would be no civil war. In fact, he gave few speeches. State and county party officials did most of the campaigning for him. Very little campaigning took place in the South, since the Republicans did not expect many votes from the slave states. (In fact, Lincoln's name did not even appear on the ballot in nine Southern states.)

Meanwhile, the Democrats were split in 1860. When Douglas received the party nomination at the convention, Southern states walked out, refusing to endorse the Northerner who had supported popular sovereignty. Instead, Southern Democrats selected John C. Breckinridge. Others threw their support to candidate John Bell, who ran on the ticket for the Constitutional Union Party, a group of Southerners who were opposed to secession.

When the election was held in November, Lincoln managed a narrow win. He polled 1,865,000 votes, which accounted for only 39 percent of the total vote, even as he gained 180 electoral votes. Breckenridge took 848,000 votes (18 percent), along with 72 electoral votes. Bell won 590,000 (12 percent), with 39 electoral votes. Ironically, Douglas came in second in the race for the popular vote, with 1,380,000 votes, yet managed to win only 12 electoral votes. Douglas received few Southern votes, and many of his Northern votes did not gain him electoral votes, as Lincoln won most of those states. With the Democrats split so dramatically, Lincoln's win was fairly assured.

THE LINCOLN PRESIDENCY

In the days following Lincoln's election in November 1860, the country began to fall apart at the seams. States began to secede from the Union, starting with South Carolina in December. By the time Lincoln took office in March 1861, 6 additional states had seceded. In all, 11 states left the Union by early summer 1861. Difficult days lay ahead for President Lincoln.

During his inauguration speech on March 4, Lincoln spoke to the Southern states in secession. He assured them that, as president, he had no plans to interfere with Southern slavery where it existed (a right he recognized under the Constitution). He appealed to the Southern states to return to the Union and reminded Southerners that they, as citizens of the United States, shared a history with the North. Lincoln said in his speech that

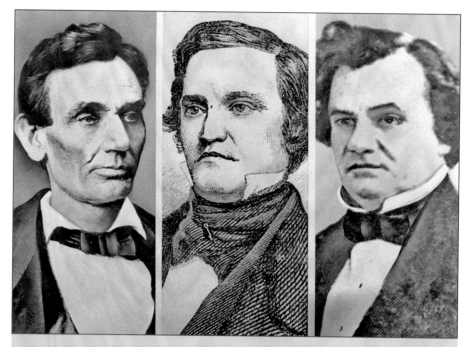

Divisions within the Democratic Party allowed Lincoln (left) to win the presidential election of 1860. Split into two groups, Southern Democrats supported John C. Breckinridge (center), while Northern Democrats favored Senator Stephen A. Douglas (right). Although Lincoln easily won the majority of electoral votes, as well as the popular vote, he did not win any Southern states.

Americans were all bound by, as noted by historian Geoffrey Ward, the "mystic chords of memory, stretching from every battlefield and patriot grave to every living heart . . . over this broad land." While appealing for the South's return, Lincoln also announced to the Southern states that he did not wish for war and that his desire was to hold the Union together.

Lincoln was soon concerned about the federal forts in Southern states. He announced he would supply food and provisions to one in need—Fort Sumter in Charleston Harbor, South Carolina. Rather than allow the fort to be resupplied, Confederate forces bombarded the island fort on April 12, 1861. These were the first shots fired of the Civil War.

With the war on, Lincoln called up state militia troops to defend the Union. He also called for 75,000 men to enlist for military duty. Lincoln ordered a blockade of all Southern ports, but the U.S. Navy did not include enough ships for the blockade to be immediately effective.

Some of Lincoln's early decisions were controversial. He authorized military spending before Congress approved it. He arrested alleged Confederate sympathizers and held them without trial. One of Lincoln's immediate concerns was a war strategy. He received much pressure to order the U.S. Army to march south from Washington, D.C., to the new Confederate capital of Richmond, Virginia, just 100 miles (160 km) away. Lincoln gave in to this expectation, and Union and Confederate troops faced one another in the first significant battle of the war: Bull Run (also known as Manassas), in Virginia, on July 21, 1861. When the Union forces lost the battle, it became clear that this war was not going to be easily won.

Lincoln spent three years searching for a general who could defeat the Southern states. He first chose General George B. McClellan in the summer of 1861 to lead the Army of the Potomac, the largest Union army in the eastern theater throughout the entire war. McClellan proved efficient in organizing the army, but ineffective in battle.

McClellan did claim victory in the Battle of Antietam, fought on September 17, 1862, the bloodiest single day of the war. Some historians maintain that the battle was only fought to a standstill, though. Either way, it would be McClellan's last as commander of the Army of the Potomac. McClellan's cautiousness in battle angered Lincoln. Other battles had proven disasters for the North, as well as others to follow: McClellan's bungled campaign on the Virginia peninsula (May to June 1862); Second Bull Run (August 1862); Fredericksburg (December 1862); and Chancellorsville (May 1863).

After McClellan had failed to aggressively pursue the retreating Confederate troops at Antietam, Lincoln replaced him

with another general, Ambrose Burnside. From May 1862 until
May 1863, Lincoln relied on four different generals—McClellan,
John Pope, Burnside, and Joseph Hooker—to command his Army
of the Potomac against the South's most capable commander,

"A New Birth of Freedom"

Throughout more than two years of war, Southern armies managed to repeatedly defeat and, in some cases, absolutely humiliate
Union forces on the battlefield. Then, during the first three days of
July 1863, the Union's Army of the Potomac finally defeated Lee
in a hard-fought battle south of the sleepy Pennsylvania town of
Gettysburg. The Confederate loss at Gettysburg would prove to be
a turning point in the war.

The battle also produced incredibly high casualties, a total of
51,000 or so between the two armies. With so many killed during
the three-day fight, Congress decided to establish a national cemetery at Gettysburg where the brave Union dead could be buried.
Later that year, on November 19, the cemetery was scheduled to
be dedicated. President Lincoln traveled to the dedication to give
a short speech. He was not the main speaker of the day. That honor
had been given to the former governor of Massachusetts, Edward
Everett, who was known for his flowery speeches. Lincoln had only
been asked to say a few words.

A crowd of 6,000 people gathered at the cemetery to hear the
speeches. Everett spoke first, his speech lasting nearly two hours.
During the speech, Lincoln sat at the speaker's stand, rephras-
ing his own speech. When he finally rose to make his delivery, he
would give one of the greatest speeches in U.S. history, the Gettysburg Address:

> Fourscore and seven years ago our fathers brought forth on this
> continent a new nation, conceived in liberty, and dedicated to
> the proposition that all men are created equal.

General Robert E. Lee. General Lee managed to defeat each general, in every case with fewer men and materiel.

President Lincoln took advantage of the single Northern victory at Antietam to issue an announcement concerning

> Now we are engaged in a great civil war, testing whether that nation, or any nation so conceived and so dedicated, can long endure. We are met on a great battlefield of that war. We have come to dedicate a portion of that field as a final resting place for those who here gave their lives that the nation might live. It is altogether fitting and proper that we should do this.
>
> But, in a larger sense, we can not dedicate—we can not consecrate—we can not hallow—this ground. The brave men, living and dead, who struggled here, have consecrated it, far above our poor power to add or detract. The world will little note, nor long remember, what we say here, but it can never forget what they did here. It is for us the living, rather, to be dedicated here to the unfinished work which they who fought here have thus far so nobly advanced. It is rather for us to be here dedicated to the great task remaining before us—that from these honored dead we take increased devotion to that cause for which they gave the last full measure of devotion—that we here highly resolve that these dead shall not have died in vain—that this nation, under God, shall have a new birth of freedom—and that government of the people, by the people, for the people, shall not perish from the earth.

The speech was no more than 270 or so words and had not taken but a couple of minutes to deliver. Following Everett's grand presentation, Lincoln's efforts seemed lacking. Even the president was disappointed with his performance, telling a friend, as noted by historian Ward, "That speech won't scour." But he had expressed grand themes through memorable phrases, creating a masterpiece of a modern speech. Although Lincoln may have thought his efforts had failed that day, Edward Everett did not. During the days that followed the dedication of the cemetery at Gettysburg, he sent the president a letter, stating, as Ward noted: "I should be glad if I could flatter myself that I came as near to the central idea of the occasion, in two hours, as you did in two minutes."

slavery. He declared that the slaves in all rebellious or seceded states were to be freed as of January 1, 1863. This noble document did not attempt to end slavery but it did add to the official motivations for the war. Northerners were always, at least in part, fighting a war against the South, which would ultimately free black slaves. Now, Lincoln was intending to fight a war for two more largely framed reasons—restoring the Union and emancipating slaves. This decision was met with some hostility across the North, but it served as the beginning of the process of eliminating slavery from U.S. soil. By January 1865, Congress passed the Thirteenth Amendment to the Constitution, ending slavery in the United States. Individual states would ratify the amendment by December.

Lincoln was often criticized during the war, as Union armies lost major battles and commanders appeared to be useless on the battlefield. Newspapers jeered and condemned Lincoln's leadership, especially following disastrous losses on the battlefield. Yet the president doggedly remained true to his goal of bringing the Union together again.

Personally, Lincoln and his family suffered much tragedy during the war. The four-year conflict preoccupied him day and night, putting enormous psychological, emotional, and physical strains on him as well as on his family. Mary Todd Lincoln was under constant suspicion from Lincoln's critics, since she was a Southerner from Kentucky whose family owned slaves. She had several brothers who served in the Confederacy. In February 1862, Lincoln's son William died. The Lincolns were deeply grieved by the loss, and the president was so sorrowful that he visited his son's mausoleum and opened his casket on two occasions so he could once more look at Willie's face.

VICTORY AT LAST

Finally, a turning point in the war came: the victory in July 1863 at Gettysburg, Pennsylvania, and the fall of Vicksburg on the

Mississippi River to another Union army under the command of Ulysses S. Grant. After the successful Northern victory at Gettysburg, Lincoln attended the dedication of a national cemetery in that small Pennsylvania town. It was there that he delivered his Gettysburg Address, explaining that this nation would have a new birth of freedom. With this speech, Americans began to think of their country as a nation rather than as a union. No longer would any state seriously consider secession from the United States.

By 1864, the war was turning in favor of the North. Through the efforts of General Grant, General Lee and the Confederacy were ultimately defeated in the spring of 1865. But the joy of victory for the North was dampened by the tragic assassination of Lincoln by an embittered Southerner named John Wilkes Booth, an actor in Washington, D.C. Sadly, the president who had guided his people through the worst conflict the United States has ever seen was himself one of the war's final casualties.

Jefferson Davis

Few American leaders ever held a more difficult role during wartime than did Jefferson Davis, the only president of the Confederate States of America. His time in office lasted just over four years, including every day of the Civil War. After years of public service to the U.S. government in the military, as a cabinet member, a U.S. representative, and a U.S. senator, Davis then accepted the responsibility that would define his life's legacy. He took on the executive responsibilities of leading 11 independent-minded Southern states, each anticipating it would hold a significant level of political power next to what was planned as a small central Confederate government.

Davis accepted the challenges that came with leading his government in a war against an enemy that consisted of fellow Americans. He took on the duties and difficulties of guiding his nation through its military conflict without enough resources or finances, even as the Confederacy's opponent had almost unlimited monies, manpower, and military material at its own disposal. As the Confederate president, Davis was criticized at almost every turn by those he had allied himself alongside against the political will of the North.

Still, the sum of his legacy is not that his country ultimately witnessed defeat in that war and an end to the political experiment of the Confederacy. Rather, his legacy is that he managed to hold together the crazy quilt of that loose political alliance of states for as long as he did.

SOUTHERN BORN

Like Abraham Lincoln, Jefferson Davis was a Kentuckian by birth. Born on June 3, 1808, he was the last of a string of 10 children born to Samuel Emory Davis and Jane Cook Davis. Young Jefferson's grandfather, Evan Davis, had immigrated to the United States from Wales during the 1700s and had made his home as a Southerner, both in Virginia and Maryland.

Samuel Davis and several of his brothers had fought in the Continental Army against the British during the Revolutionary War. He served for a time in a Georgia cavalry unit and also fought as an infantry officer during the British siege of Savannah. Three of Jefferson Davis's older brothers fought the British as well during service in the War of 1812. Two of them served directly under General Andrew Jackson and participated in the Battle of New Orleans. As for young Jefferson, he would have to wait for his military service, but he would eventually participate in three wars: the Black Hawk War, the Mexican-American War, and the Civil War.

The family did not remain in Kentucky during Jefferson's childhood. When Jefferson was only three years old, the family moved to St. Mary Parish in Louisiana. Then, after his older brother Joseph moved to Mississippi to operate a plantation, his father moved the rest of the family there as well. Young Jefferson was just four at the time. The Davis family's new home was in Wilkinson County, Mississippi, not far from the frontier town of Woodville.

Jefferson's formal education began early, at age five, when he and his sister Mary began attending Wilkinson Academy, a school situated in a log cabin about a mile from their home. After two years, young Jefferson was enrolled in a Catholic school, St. Thomas at St. Rose Priory, an institution led by Dominican monks. At the time he attended, seven-year-old Jefferson Davis was the only Protestant student.

His schooling continued into his teen years. He attended Jefferson College, located in Washington, Mississippi, at age 10. At age 13, he enrolled in Transylvania University in Lexington, Kentucky. When he was 16, Jefferson received an appointment from President James Monroe to the U.S. Military Academy at West Point, entering at an age younger than most cadets. He remained at West Point for four years until he graduated. He did not perform well at the academy, earning low grades compared to other students. However, he received high praise from at least one of his fellow classmates, as noted by historian Felicity Allen: "He was distinguished in his corps for manly bearing and high-toned and lofty character. His figure was very soldier like and rather robust; his step springy, resembling the tread of an Indian brave on the war-path."

Cadet Jefferson Davis, graduating class of 1828, did not have to wait long to prove his military qualities. He was immediately assigned to the 1st Infantry, commissioned as a second lieutenant. His unit was posted in the remote regions of the Wisconsin Territory at Fort Howard, moving to Fort Crawford by 1829. His first assignment at Fort Crawford was to organize and supervise further construction of the fort by leading timber-cutting crews along the banks of the Red Cedar River. Later in 1829, he was reassigned to a new post at Fort Winnebago, where he supervised the building of a sawmill on the local Yellow River. When he caught pneumonia in 1831, he became quite ill and needed to be assigned back to Fort Crawford.

Davis's first true military experience began in 1831 with the opening of the Black Hawk War, a Native American conflict led

Future Confederate president Jefferson Davis served in the military during the Black Hawk War. After the Battle of Bad Axe (above) in Wisconsin, Davis was assigned to accompany Native American leader Black Hawk to prison. Black Hawk, treated favorably by Davis, spoke well of the Southern leader in his autobiography.

by the well-known Chief Black Hawk. The war took Davis and the 1st Infantry to Illinois Country, where he and a detachment of soldiers helped remove white miners from disputed Native American land. The war continued until 1833, and Lieutenant Davis participated in several engagements, including the decisive Battle of Bad Axe. In time, Chief Black Hawk surrendered and was taken prisoner. Davis's commanding officer, Colonel Zachary Taylor (who would later serve as a leading general in the Mexican-American War, as well as U.S. president), assigned him to escort the defeated chief to prison. During the march, Davis treated Black Hawk so well that the chief took a liking to the young lieutenant, who helped turn Black Hawk from leading further uprisings against the United States.

The war ended in 1833, and Davis was soon assigned to yet another post, this time to a new cavalry regiment, the 1st

Dragoons. He also received a promotion to first lieutenant. Between 1833 and 1835, Jefferson Davis continued fighting Native Americans, including those found farther out on the Great Plains, such as the Pawnee and the Comanche.

RESIGNED BY LOVE

By the mid-1830s, Jefferson Davis had fought in several conflicts against Native Americans and advanced in rank as an officer. But after seven years of military service, he suddenly resigned from the U.S. Army. Several family members, including an influential uncle, had begun to suggest to Davis that he might not want to continue to "waste" his life as a soldier. They encouraged him to leave the military and pursue a career as a civilian, thinking him an exceptionally talented young man.

Another main reason for his resignation was a woman, who happened to be the daughter of Zachary Taylor, then the commander of the 1st Infantry. Davis had fallen in love with Sarah Knox Taylor, and although she returned his affections, her father did not approve. Under the circumstances, Davis could not reasonably remain under Taylor's command and marry his daughter, so he resigned his commission. The two married on June 17, 1835.

The marriage, sadly, did not last long. The new couple prepared to settle down and raise cotton as prospering planters. Then the two were struck with malaria during a visit to Jefferson Davis's oldest sister in Louisiana. Davis recovered, but his new bride of only three months died. The loss was devastating for the future leader of the Confederacy.

By early 1836, he had moved to Brierfield Plantation in Warren County, Mississippi. During the next eight years, Jefferson Davis largely lived a life of lonely quiet, staying away from people, spending much of his time overseeing his plantation and its slaves and consuming long hours with study as he poured himself into his books on history, economics, government, constitutional law, and politics. His brother Joseph was a frequent visitor. Although Davis's grief deeply marked this period of time in his life, these years also helped prepare him for much of the life's work that would place his mark on U.S. history. During these same years, Davis became wealthy through extensive cotton cultivation.

By 1843, he turned to politics. He was selected as a delegate to the Democratic convention, where he gave several speeches and made solid impressions on his fellow attendees. Soon he was receiving invitations to speak publicly. By the following year, Davis was chosen as a state elector for the Democratic Party candidate, a Tennessean named James K. Polk. At this point in his political thinking, Davis saw himself as a strict interpreter of the U.S. Constitution and a strong advocate for states' rights and limited federal power. He also supported the annexation of Texas into the Union. The following year, he won a seat in the U.S. House of Representatives, kicking off his career as an elected political figure.

LOVE AND WAR

The same year he took office as a representative from the state of Mississippi, Jefferson Davis also experienced another change in his life. Ten years after his first marriage had ended tragically, Davis remarried. This time it was to Varina Howell, whose grandfather, Richard Howell, had served as governor of New Jersey. Davis had met Governor Howell the previous year, but Howell had died in the meantime. Varina's family members were fellow Mississippians who owned a plantation called the Briars outside Natchez. Davis and his new wife remained happily married for many years, and she ultimately outlived him. Through the years, they had six children together, four boys and two girls. The youngest, Varina Anne, whom everyone called Winnie, became known later in life as the "Daughter of the Confederacy."

Jefferson Davis began his work in Congress during an exciting time in U.S. history. The slavery issue, which centered on the westward expansion of slavery, was a constant subject of debate and political squabbling between Northern and Southern congressmen. Texas was admitted into the Union in 1845. There were considerations regarding the annexation of the Oregon Country (the modern-day states of Oregon, Washington, and Idaho) and the further expansion of the American frontier. Through the debates and speeches, Davis presented himself as a loyal American, one who believed strongly in the future of the great republic. He expressed strong loyalties toward the Union. These would become, in part, ironic positions for Davis when he joined the Confederacy 15 years later.

By 1846, a new debate was on the floor: a possible war with Mexico. Hostilities were expanding between the two countries due to the annexing of Texas, a former Mexican province that had revolted during the 1830s and gained its independence from Mexico. Davis favored a war with Mexico, and he had also favored the annexation of Texas, knowing that war might result. While still a representative, Davis was selected to command the 1st Mississippi Regiment of Riflemen. When war officially began between the two countries in 1846, Davis knew what he must do. Certain he could have a greater impact on events as a soldier than as a U.S. representative, Davis resigned from Congress and joined his regiment in New Orleans.

Davis soon attached his riflemen to the main body of U.S. troops stationed along the Rio Grande, those serving under the command of General Zachary Taylor, Davis's former father-in-law. The 1st Mississippi would prove itself well in the coming action. Davis took such a hands-on approach to the unit, that he managed to arm them with the latest percussion cap rifles and had even written up a military manual for his men. With his West Point experience, he drilled his men and trained the officers under his command.

Davis and his men would be among General Taylor's top regiments. In late September 1846, Davis and the Mississippi riflemen participated in the charge against Monterey, successfully capturing Fort Teneria. Over the days that followed, the 1st Mississippi, along with units from Tennessee, drove Mexican forces from several smaller hilltop forts and other positions, gaining Davis the attention of his superiors.

But Davis made his greatest contribution to the Mexican-American War during the Battle of Buena Vista. He led his riflemen and some volunteers from Indiana into the fight, causing a wing of Mexico's army to turn in the face of a bold frontal assault by the Americans. Immediately following this field success, Davis and his men came under attack by a brigade of Mexican lancers on horseback riding hard at the Mississippi riflemen. Davis quickly ordered his men into a defensive "V" formation with ravines at each flank, causing the lancers to gallop straight into a withering fire. Later that same day, Davis and his men, despite having taken serious casualties, successfully smashed into the Mexican right flank, causing it to crumble. At that point in the battle, Colonel Davis took a serious wound in the foot but remained in the action until the fight was over.

When General Taylor wrote his after-battle report, he gave special mention to Jefferson Davis, exalting his courage and coolness under fire. Seeing Davis in a new light, Taylor is reported to have admitted, according to historian Holman Hamilton: "My daughter, sir, was a better judge of men than I was." The 1st Mississippi remained active through to the war's end in the summer of 1847. Davis's contribution to the country's military effort gained him the rank of brigadier general of a Mississippi brigade, which President Polk himself offered him. But the states' rights advocate turned down the offer, believing his appointment was unconstitutional. He felt the U.S. Constitution empowered the states, not the federal government, to appoint militia officers.

RENEWED POLITICAL CAREER

Colonel Davis and his riflemen returned to Mississippi in July 1847. Davis may have surrendered his seat in the House of Representatives to join the war effort, but he would quickly return to political office. The governor of Mississippi was well aware of Davis's military success and in August selected him to serve the remainder of Senator Jesse Speight's term, as Speight had died. Just months after returning from the war, Davis was back in Washington. He would in time be appointed as the chairman of the Senate Committee on Military Affairs. (He was also selected as a regent to the new Smithsonian Institution.)

Over the next four years, Senator Davis would hold a ringside seat to the major political events of his time, events that would ultimately lead the United States closer to civil war. His former father-in-law and commander, Zachary Taylor, was elected president in 1848. Controversy began between Southerners and Northerners in Congress over the admission of California as a free state. (California was part of the territory gained by the United States after winning the Mexican-American War.) Senator Davis opposed the compromise drawn up by Kentucky senator Henry Clay and spoke out several times against it. In doing so, Davis aligned himself against Clay and alongside an aging South Carolina senator and former vice president, John C. Calhoun, a strong supporter of slavery.

Davis suggested an alternative to the compromise: that the western regions of the United States be divided by the same longitudinal line established in the early 1820s to divide the Louisiana Territory between slave and free regions. He felt the line had already been established and accepted by Congress a generation earlier and could easily be extended farther westward. But when the vote was taken, it failed with 24 votes in favor (all cast by Southerners) and 32 opposed.

Davis was immediately concerned about the vote and its outcome. Congress had, technically, denied that the line established 30 years earlier applied to the West as well. Neverthe-less, at this point in his political career, just a decade away from the Civil War, Jefferson Davis did not align himself with any advocates of secession. As he would later write in his memoirs:

> My devotion to the Union of our fathers had been so often and so publicly declared; I had on the floor of the Senate so defiantly challenged any question of my fidelity to it; my services, civil and military, had now extended through so long a period and were so generally known, that I felt quite assured that no whisperings of envy or ill-will could lead the people of Mississippi to believe that I had dishon-ored their trust by using the power they had conferred on me to destroy the government to which I was accredited. Then, as afterward, I regarded the separation of the States as a great, though not the greater evil.

When Congress accepted the Compromise of 1850 despite the misgivings and opposition of most Southern members, Davis could not support the direction it signaled for slavery's fu-ture in the West. He soon resigned his Senate seat to become the candidate for the States' Rights Democrats in the forthcoming election, which took place later that same year. The incumbent, Governor Quitman of Mississippi, had already been nominated for another term, but he withdrew his nomination, feeling he could not be reelected. Senator Davis soon took his place. How-ever, his nomination and the election were only six weeks apart, and Davis turned up sick, unable to even leave his plantation home. Due to the senator's popularity as a strong supporter of states' rights, he lost the election by fewer than 1,000 votes to his fellow senator, Henry Foote.

With the gubernatorial election behind him, Davis re-tired, ready to throw himself back into the private planter life. He did remain active in his state's politics, however, taking part in a states' rights convention in Jackson in 1852. He also cam-paigned across the South on behalf of Democratic presidential

Jefferson Davis returned to public office as a member of the U.S. Senate after lead-
ing a regiment during the Mexican-American War. Representing Mississippi, Davis
served in the Senate during one of the most tumultuous eras of U.S. history. Davis
continued his political career as President Franklin Pierce's secretary of war and
another term in the Senate before becoming president of the Confederacy.

candidate Franklin Pierce. When Pierce was elected president, public service came calling at Davis's door again, as the new chief executive appointed the Mississippi politician as his secretary of war.

Davis threw himself whole-heartedly into his new Washington role. He increased the size of the army during his years in office and introduced a new system of infantry tactics. He personally oversaw the adoption of new and improved weapons for the army. He sent military engineering expeditions into the far west to examine possible routes for a transcontinental railroad stretching from the Mississippi River to the Pacific coast. Under his guidance, the army even experimented with camels for use out in remote desert posts.

Pierce served only one term, as the Democratic Party nomination was handed off to James Buchanan. Davis finished his work as secretary of war in 1857. In the meantime, Davis had been elected to the Senate in 1856, and was soon serving the Union in the halls of Congress rather than the Department of War.

Events were moving quickly across the country. By the late 1850s, there was a more threatening possibility than ever of Southern states seceding from the Union over limitations on slavery's expansion across the West. North and South were locked in constant feuding over slavery and whether people in the West had the right to vote down slavery, a right that came to be known as popular sovereignty. Then, an 1857 Supreme Court decision, *Dred Scott v. Sandford*, struck down the Missouri Compromise, which had limited the existence of slavery in the northern portions of the old Louisiana Purchase Territory.

The nation seemed bound for even greater conflict in the future. Even then, Senator Davis still did not pursue secession. During the summer of 1858, while spending the season in New England, Davis gave a speech onboard a ship in Boston Harbor on the Fourth of July. In his address, he spoke against secession as a political alternative. On October 11, he delivered another speech in which he again urged Americans to remain together and preserve the Union.

It was not that Davis, a strong supporter of states' rights, did not believe the states had the right to secede at their choice. However, if any Southern states chose to secede over the slavery issue and go their own way, Davis did not believe that the federal government would simply lie down and let them go without a fight. From his experience as secretary of war, he was well aware that the South was not equipped for extended military action in the form of a civil war against the North. For the moment, even into the late 1850s, Jefferson Davis continued to stand strongly against secession by the Southern states.

ELECTION AND SECESSION

Despite the reluctance of influential Southerners to support secession, the year 1860 brought a change regarding the political future of the South. Abraham Lincoln was elected president in November, signaling to the Southern secessionists that the time for separation from the Union had arrived. Lincoln, although not an abolitionist, was believed to favor ending slavery and certainly had declared himself an enemy of expanding slavery into the western territories. Many Southerners saw things as being on a radical course toward destructing their way of life, including slavery, and states began taking steps toward secession. South Carolina led the way, voting in a December 1860 convention to secede from the Union. As for Davis's Mississippi, it made a similar move the following month. Once his state had voted for secession, Davis felt he had no choice but to make a farewell address to his fellow senators and resign, soon to return to Mississippi.

Although Davis had opposed secession, he accepted it as fact for his state and took immediate steps to participate in any military conflict that might develop. With his military experience, he anticipated being asked to lead the Confederate military. He was mistaken. A convention held in Montgomery, Alabama, instead chose Davis to be the president of the Confederate states.

On February 10, 1861, Davis and his wife, Varina, were home at Brierfield, their plantation south of Vicksburg. They were out in the garden pruning roses when Davis received the telegram informing him he had been picked for the presidency. Varina noted his appearance as he received the news, as historian Geoffrey Ward quoted: "Reading that telegram, he looked so grieved that I feared some evil had befallen our family. After a few minutes, he told me [what it contained], as a man might speak of a sentence of death."

Jefferson, the military veteran, public servant, and political figure, understood as much as any man could have the responsibilities that lay before him. He was to provide the leadership for a political experiment: a conservative government based around states' rights. There was a danger that no one would be able or willing to lead such a loose organization of independent states. Even Davis's own wife knew his political and personal limits, as Geoffrey Ward noted: "He did not know the arts of a politician and would not practice them if understood." But Davis took the task placed before him.

Eight days after receiving the telegram, Davis was in Montgomery taking his oath of office, a six-year term under the new constitution of the Confederate States of America. (To date, Davis had never completed a single term of political office, and his term as Confederate president would prove no different.) After his swearing-in, he spoke to the assembled crowd, recalled by historian Ward:

> Our present political position has been achieved in a manner unprecedented in the history of nations. It illustrates the American idea that governments rest on the consent

of the governed, and that it is the right of the governed,
and that it is the right of the people to alter or abolish
them at will whenever they become destructive of the
ends for which they were established . . . Obstacles may
retard, but they can not long prevent, the progress of a
movement sanctified by its justice and sustained by a vir-
tuous people.

At the conclusion of his address, the throng of well-wishers
cheered their new president and began singing "Farewell to the
Star-Spangled Banner," and a popular minstrel tune, "Dixie's
Land."

PRESIDENT DAVIS AND THE WAR

Although Southern states had seceded from the Union, Davis
and others in both the North and the South hoped a war between the states could still be avoided. To that end, Davis immediately established a commission to negotiate with the federal
government over any issues that complicated the departure of
the South. One of the primary sticking points was the existence
of federal military and civilian installations, such as forts and
lighthouses, on Southern soil. The commission was sent to
Washington, D.C., in March, but its members were not authorized by Davis to negotiate the return of the Southern states
back into the Union.

In the meantime, Davis prepared for war, selecting General
P.G.T. Beauregard as the commander of Confederate troops in
Charleston, South Carolina. A federal installation, Fort Sumter,
stood in Charleston's harbor. By early April, the commander of
Sumter had refused to turn over the fort to state officials, so
President Davis and his cabinet approved bombarding the fort.
This move guaranteed a civil war.

As the war began, Virginia finally seceded after cautious de-
lays. This led Davis to move the capital of the Confederacy from
Montgomery to Richmond, Virginia, just 100 miles (160 km)

Jefferson Davis was inaugurated in Montgomery, Alabama, the first official capital of the Confederacy. After three months, however, Southern leaders decided to relocate government headquarters to the larger city of Richmond, Virginia. This move essentially saved Alabama from devastation, as Federal troops targeted Richmond. Above, now known as the White House of the Confederacy, the Executive Mansion was home to Davis and his family while the Confederacy was in Richmond.

from Washington, D.C. With this move, much of the significant action of the war over the next four years would take place in Virginia.

Since the war, historians have wrestled over whether Jefferson Davis was the right man to lead the Confederacy as its president. Some have been extremely critical of his political style and personality. He has been accused of giving too much time and attention to small details. It is certain that he did not surround himself with a large number of advisers, but instead chose to rely on only a handful, leaving himself to make many

Davis's Life After the Civil War

After leading the South through the Civil War, Davis was captured in May 1865 and held in a military prison for two years while the U.S. Congress and American public opinion wrestled with what to do with the former Confederate president. In 1866, he was charged with treason, but the case was finally dropped in February 1869. In the meantime, while in prison, Davis arranged the sale of his Mississippi plantation to one of his former slaves.

Between 1867 and 1869, Davis, released from prison on bail, visited Canada, Cuba (whose purchase he had always supported as president of the Confederacy), and Europe. By 1869, with the charges against him finally dropped, Davis took a job as president of the Carolina Life Insurance Company, based in Memphis. When Robert E. Lee died in 1870, Davis presided over the memorial ceremonies. Although he managed to get himself elected again to the U.S. Senate in 1875, he was denied his office under the new Fourteenth Amendment to the Constitution. When an offer was made to make him president of the Agriculture and Mechanical College of Texas (today's Texas A&M University), he refused the appointment.

In 1877, he paid a visit to England, then returned the following year to Beauvoir, his estate outside Biloxi, Mississippi. Through the next three years, he penned a manuscript, *The Rise and Fall of the Confederate Government*. After another trip to Europe, he returned home to write another book, *A Short History of the Confederate States of America*, which he finally completed in the fall of 1889.

He did not live to see that work in print. On December 6, he died in New Orleans at the age of 81. The cause of death was never established. His funeral was one of the grandest and largest ever for an American Southerner. Jefferson Davis was buried in Hollywood Cemetery in Richmond, the capital of the Confederate government he had served as president.

decisions. He could be extremely aloof and removed with most people. According to historian Ward, former Texas governor Sam Houston once stated he thought Davis was "cold as a lizard." Davis was so formal that he typically refused to use anyone's first names, even when referring to his own slaves. Davis could be high-strung and nervous, unable to sleep. During the war, he never managed to raise the money needed to provide enough supplies, food, uniforms, and pay to the Confederate Army, but it is unlikely that any other person could have done much better as president of the Rebel states.

One of Davis's most important moves as Confederate president was to replace General Joseph Johnston, who commanded the Army of Northern Virginia. In Johnston's place Davis appointed Robert E. Lee, who would prove himself as the South's most capable military commander. The change was made in June 1862, and Lee remained his army's leader through the remainder of the war. Most of the South's greatest victories in the East must be credited to the brilliant tactics of Robert E. Lee. General Lee and Davis generally kept up a good working relationship during the war, but Davis never turned over the entire direction of the Southern strategy to Lee. Davis continuously made the primary strategic decisions for his military on his own or gave final approval to Lee's suggestions.

Davis stuck with Lee in the East even after the successful Virginia general lost a major battle at Gettysburg, Pennsylvania, in July 1863. When Lee offered his resignation, Davis refused it. Lee's fortunes of war eventually ran out, and the wily Southern commander found himself boxed in at Petersburg, Virginia, south of Richmond, by the early summer of 1864. While Lee remained in Petersburg, Richmond and Davis's government remained secure. But when Union troops broke the siege in April 1865, President Davis was forced to flee for his life to Danville, Virginia, along with members of his cabinet. Over the following days, Davis found his way to Greensboro, North Carolina, where he soon received the news he had always dreaded:

Lee had surrendered to General Grant at Appomattox Court House.

The news reached Davis on April 12, and he met with his cabinet for the final time on May 5, 1865, in Georgia. At that time, the Confederate government was officially disbanded. Five days later, Davis was captured in Irwin County and spent two years in a prison cell at Fort Monroe, Virginia. Through his leadership, President Davis had managed to keep the Confederate government afloat for four years. Through those difficult years, he struggled to carry out his duties as the South's chief executive. But the Southern states constantly blocked his actions on their behalf and were thus hurt by the very independence they had asserted when they seceded from the United States in the first place. Ironically, Davis had always supported states' rights. By demanding a weak national government, the states of the Confederacy not only complicated the work of their president, but also worked against any potential to ultimately win the war. Jefferson Davis himself once observed that, should the Confederacy fail and die, its tombstone should read, "Died of a theory," recalled historian Ward. No one came to understand the truth of that prediction more than Jefferson Davis himself.

Robert E. Lee

Robert E. Lee was born on January 19, 1807, in Virginia, the state that his colonial ancestors had helped establish. His birthplace was one of his mother's family homes, Stratford Hall Plantation in Virginia's Westmoreland County, where his parents had married in the Great Hall on a hot day in 1793. Lee was the fifth child of a hero of the Revolutionary War. His father was the military leader Henry Lee, whom everyone referred to as "Lighthorse Harry." His mother was Anne Hill Carter, a member of one of Virginia's prestigious planter families. Her great grandfather Robert "King" Carter, who died in 1732, is thought to have been the wealthiest man in the colonies.

A STURDY VIRGINIAN

As wealthy as the Carter family might have been, Lighthorse Harry was not so fortunate. By the time of Robert's birth, Henry Lee had become known for his bad business dealings and his carelessness with money. When young Robert was two years old, his father was clapped into debtor's prison. In time, the elder Lee left his family. As noted by historian Gary W. Gallagher, "Harry Lee had not been able to exercise self-control or take care of his family, and so he abandoned them." He died when Robert was 11 years old.

Despite the failings of her husband, Anne Carter Lee went to great lengths to raise her children with values she held as important. For Robert, those included a strong sense of honor and duty. Although she had few financial resources at her disposal, Anne Lee made certain that Robert was as well educated as possible.

At age 18, Robert E. Lee received a commission to attend the U.S. Military Academy at West Point. Moving to upstate New York on the Hudson River, Lee found cadet life challenging. Still, he managed to become the first West Point cadet to make sergeant by the end of his first year. His solid academic studies, along with his strong character development, helped him through his four years at the academy, and in 1829 he graduated second in his class of 46 cadets. Lee's graduation from military school was marred by the death of his mother, who passed away just weeks later from tuberculosis.

Lee's academic success tells only part of his story at West Point. He also managed to complete his four years of study without receiving a single demerit, which is a note against a cadet marking him with some sort of wrongdoing. This is an achievement that is almost unheard of at the military school. (Union general William Tecumseh Sherman also attended West Point, and he received 150 demerits *each year!*)

Discipline and self-motivation did not keep Lee from socializing at the academy or from making lifelong friends. Lee was so popular among his fellow cadets that they appointed him as cadet adjutant during his senior year, the highest leadership role among West Point cadets. Fellow classmate Joseph Johnston would one day fight alongside Lee during the Civil

War. He admired Cadet Lee so much that he would later remark of him, according to historian Brian Sobel: "No other youth or man so united the qualities that win warm friendship and command high respect. For he was full of sympathy and kindness . . . while his correctness of demeanor and attention to all duties . . . gave him a superiority that everyone acknowledged in his heart."

LEE THE ENGINEER

With the completion of his studies at West Point, and given his high class rank, Robert E. Lee had his choice of how to serve in the U.S. Army. He could have chosen several fields, including that of a dashing cavalry officer or artilleryman. Instead, the newly commissioned brevet second lieutenant chose to join the Corps of Engineers.

Throughout the 1830s, Lee was assigned to various locations across the young American republic, where he worked on military engineering and water projects, including Cockspur Island's Fort Pulaski and Hampton Roads's Fort Monroe and Fort Calhoun. Between 1834 and 1837, Lee was assigned as assistant to the chief engineer in Washington, D.C. During that time, he helped survey the state line between Ohio and the new state of Michigan.

Out in frontier St. Louis, as a first lieutenant of engineers, Lee supervised improvement projects to control the flow of the Mississippi River, including clearing new channels, building dikes, and constructing piers along the town's waterfront. By 1840, he had been made captain. Engineering assignments in New York City during the early 1840s included Fort Hamilton, named for the nation's first secretary of the treasury, Alexander Hamilton, who had been a good friend of Lee's father.

At such postings, Lee did not simply develop engineering plans and order others to complete them. He was a hands-on engineer. Historian Douglas Southall Freeman, in his book *R.E. Lee*, noted an observation made by a local resident during Lee's time working in St. Louis. The resident recalled how Lee,

> . . . went in person with the hands every morning about sunrise, and worked day by day in the hot, broiling sun. . . . He shared in the hard task and common fare and rations furnished to the common laborers . . . He maintained and preserved under all circumstances his dignity and gentlemanly bearing, winning and commanding the esteem, regard, and respect of every one under him.

It was in 1831, during his time at Fort Monroe, Virginia, that Lee married a Virginia belle, Mary Ann Randolph Custis. Her family had connections to the family of George Washington, whom Lee admired greatly. Mary Ann was the only child of George Washington Parke Custis, grandson of Martha Washington and her first husband, Dan Custis. (Martha and George Washington did not have any children of their own.) The Lees would have seven children during their nearly 40 years of marriage. They would raise their three sons and four daughters in Arlington House, a Custis mansion and plantation that overlooked the Virginia banks of the Potomac River.

OFF TO WAR

General in chief of the U.S. Army Winfield Scott chose Lee to serve on the board of visitors at West Point, which examined cadets as they neared graduation. By 1846, having served for 17 years, plus 4 years as a cadet, Robert E. Lee was about to take on responsibilities different from any he had ever carried out as a military man. He was off to war.

In 1846, the United States and Mexico finally slid into a clash of arms, which had been threatening since the Texas Revolution in the 1830s. When the United States annexed Texas as a state, Mexico bristled, and a border dispute finally erupted into

Raised mostly by his mother, Robert E. Lee was known for his discipline, patience, and determination to succeed. After making history at the United States Military Academy at West Point by graduating without a single demerit, Lee joined the Corps of Engineers.

war. Lee would serve as an engineer during the international conflict, serving directly under General Scott as one of his aides. Lee proved himself invaluable to Scott and the U.S. military effort. As U.S. forces prepared to land at the Mexican port of Veracruz, it was Lee, along with Joe Johnston, who scouted out positions around the city for American artillery placements. It was at Veracruz that 39-year-old Captain Lee came under enemy fire for the first time.

But Lee made an even greater contribution when Mexican forces stood their ground against the American advance toward Mexico City. At Cerro Gordo (Fat Hill), Lee's scouting of the region provided Scott with information that allowed him to cut off the Mexican army's communication lines and push them from their earthen fortifications.

While scouting enemy positions, Lee moved extremely close to Mexican positions. As he was crawling near a local spring, Mexican soldiers approached and remained by the water source. For most of a day, Lee hid behind a fallen log while Mexican troops sat at the spring, unaware of his presence. He managed to get away only under cover of darkness. According to historian Brian Sobel, such exemplary work by Lee led General Scott to remark that he had developed "a fancy for Lee, whose military genius [was] far above that of any other officer in the Army." Lee's months in Mexico gained him brevet (temporary) promotions to major, lieutenant colonel, and then colonel. (Despite these field advancements, Lee's permanent rank remained captain until 1855.)

During Lee's service in Mexico, he fought alongside many military men who would play crucial roles as commanders, both Federal and Confederate, during the Civil War. It was during the Mexican conflict that such officers as Ulysses S. Grant and Thomas "Stonewall" Jackson gained their first glimpse of serious battle. The engineering corps Lee belonged to included others who would become key players in the war between the North and South. They included P.G.T. Beauregard, George B.

McClellan, Joe Johnston, and George Gordon Meade, who would defeat Lee more than 15 years later during the Battle of Gettysburg.

Following the action at Cerro Gordo, Lee went on to participate in battles at Contreras, Churubusco, and Chapultepec, where he was wounded. It was also through his war experience in Mexico that Lee gained important insights into how field battles are won and lost. He came to understand in practical terms how, in the words of historian Sobel, "a smaller army could outwork, outmaneuver, and ultimately outfight a larger force." Such lessons would serve him well during the Civil War.

BACK TO THE STATES

Following the American victory over the Mexicans in 1847, Lee spent the next three years as an engineer at Baltimore Harbor's Fort Carroll. By the early 1850s, he was appointed superintendent of West Point. Despite his successes in uniform, both during peacetime and war, Lee did not feel he was up to the challenge. As noted by historian Sobel, Lee wrote: "I fear I cannot realize [the secretary of war's] expectations in the management of an institution requiring more skill and more experience than I command."

Despite his reluctance, his three years at West Point were grand days for Lee. Much of his earlier military service had kept Lee apart from his wife and children. But at the academy, they were together. His oldest son, George Washington Custis Lee, was a cadet at the time. They lived in a large house and enjoyed the cadets, whom Lee counseled personally as a father figure. The Lees especially liked a young man named James Ewell Brown "J.E.B." Stuart, a fellow Virginian, who would serve during the Civil War as Lee's most capable cavalry officer. Another cadet who attended West Point during the years Lee was superintendent was John Bell Hood, a Texan who would serve under Lee during the Civil War.

TO THE WEST

With new orders issued in 1855, the U.S. Army again separated Lee from his family. He was assigned to Camp Cooper, Texas, outside San Antonio. He was to serve as second in command to Colonel Albert Sidney Johnston, who was the regimental commander of the 2nd U.S. Cavalry, a newly formed unit. Lee's new placement required him to leave the engineering corps, which he had served for more than 25 years. Experience told him that he would have a better opportunity for advancement in rank if he went with the cavalry rather than remaining with the engineers. The new post brought a rank of lieutenant colonel.

Despite his new rank, the post in Texas brought little advantage otherwise. He was alone, his family back in Virginia. Western duty centered on the thankless task of chasing down Comanche across the plains of Texas and modern-day Oklahoma, as well as the occasional Mexican bandit or cattle rustler. The region was a harsh, blighted land that only made Lee more nostalgic for his home back in the East.

Despite the remoteness of the posting, Texas did not represent a complete washout for Lee. Once again, as with the Mexican-American War, the middle-aged Lee served alongside others who would make their names during the Civil War. These men included such figures as George Thomas, William Hardee, Earl Van Dorn, Edmund Kirby Smith, and, once again, John Bell Hood. Although Lee never understood completely the Native American ways of fighting, he was impressed with their determination and combat skills in the face of a stronger, more numerous opponent. It was another lesson he would take into the Civil War.

Lee's assignment in Texas technically lasted for six years, from 1855 until 1861, the year the Civil War opened. But his time in the West was interrupted by the death of his father-in-law and the necessity of taking a leave of absence. He had to carry out duties as the executor of his father-in-law's estate, and Mary Ann Lee's health was in significant decline. Between 1857 and 1860,

Lee remained at Arlington. But a single event of immediate historical importance brought him back into service in 1859.

That fall, an outspoken and infamous abolitionist leader named John Brown, along with a small gang of followers, tried to ignite a slave revolt in western Virginia at Harpers Ferry. (Today, the former frontier river town lies in West Virginia.) Brown's plan had called for the seizure of the federal arsenal at Harpers Ferry, which would provide weapons with which Brown and his men (of the 21 coconspirators, 5 were black) could supply slaves and help bring about a successful uprising. But Brown's plan quickly unraveled as townspeople caught wind of the raid on their town and turned on Brown and his followers, trapping them in the town's fire engine house. When telegraph messages informed the Department of War in Washington of the raid, Lieutenant J.E.B. Stuart, who had been a favorite of Lee's during his tenure over West Point, was there. He soon carried orders from the Department of War to Lee across the Potomac at Arlington, sending Lee to Harpers Ferry.

Upon his arrival by train, Lee took control of the situation. The day following Brown's raid, the Virginia military man sent a unit of U.S. Marines forward to storm the fire engine house, despite the fact that the raiders were holding hostages. The assault, which lasted little more than three minutes, was successful in ending the attempted slave rebellion. Several of Brown's followers were killed, and he was taken prisoner. The abolitionist leader was put on trial, accused of treason against Virginia, found guilty, and hanged on December 2, 1859. In Lee's report on his operations to end the raid, he referred to Brown's plan, according to historian Clifford Dowdey, as an "attempt of a fanatic or a madman." The raid would serve as one more event during the late 1850s that would speed the coming of the Civil War.

Within months of the Brown raid, Lee was summoned back to permanent duty in Texas, with a new rank of colonel and commander of the Department of Texas. The year 1860 would be the last before the outbreak of hostilities between the North

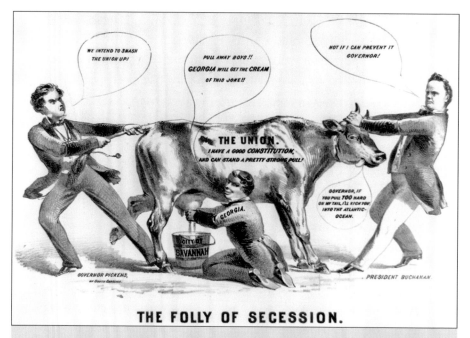

THE FOLLY OF SECESSION.

The growing furor over slavery and secession created an almost impossible situation for Robert E. Lee, a man who supported the Union and yet loved the South. Although he had served in the U.S. military for 36 years, Lee resigned his commission and sided with the Confederacy when Virginia seceded from the Union. Under his command and leadership, Rebel forces were successful in numerous battles. Above, a political cartoon depicts President Buchanan fighting over the Union with Governor Pickens of South Carolina while Georgia reaps the benefits.

and South. The Republican Party, having been established just six years earlier, was opposed to the expansion of slavery into the western territories of the United States. Democrats in the slave-holding Southern states sought the advancement of slavery into new lands. When the Republicans nominated an Illinois lawyer named Abraham Lincoln as their presidential candidate, the die was cast. Southern leaders believed Lincoln to be a supporter of abolition. Should he be elected, the South was determined to make moves toward secession from the Union.

Concerning talk of secession, Lee felt it to be not only fool-ishness, but also treason and revolution. Lee, though a Virginian, was also an American and a military man who had always been a supporter and defender of the Union. As noted by historian Brian Sobel, Lee had once penned the words: "I prize the Union very highly and know of no personal sacrifice that I would not make to preserve it, save that of honor."

Never an outspoken man politically, Lee watched as the Democratic Party split at its convention when Southern delegates walked out following the nomination of a Northerner, another man from Illinois, Senator Stephen Douglas. Lee remained on the sidelines while other Southerners nominated their own candidate, fellow Southerner John Breckinridge. Lee watched as Republican Lincoln was elected that fall, and he was hopeful that the United States would not slide toward further division. Following the election, according to historian Douglas Freeman in his biography *R.E. Lee*, the Virginia colonel wrote a letter to his son George Washington Custis Lee, concerned about what steps might follow:

> My only hope [is] for the preservation of the Union, and I will cling to it to the last. Feeling the aggressions of the North, resenting their denial of the equal rights of our citizens . . . I am [also] not pleased with the course of the "Cotton States," as they term themselves, with their selfish, dictatorial bearing. . . . While I wish to do what is right, I am unwilling to do what is wrong, either at the bidding of the South or the North.

Lee would soon find his loyalties to the United States tested, just as his letter indicated. Southern states did secede, beginning with South Carolina within weeks of the presidential election. By the early months of 1861, others followed.

WAR ON THE HORIZON

Out in Texas, Lee waited as events quickened. By February 1861, the Texas legislature voted to secede from the Union. The

The Ledger of War

As the war opened in the spring of 1861, both sides were poorly prepared for the conflict that had been so long in coming. The Confederacy went into the war lacking enough of nearly everything needed to fight a prolonged conflict, including manpower, weapons, war materiel, transportation, and even such necessities as food and clothing. During the first year of the war, the South used whatever advantages it had available.

One Southern advantage was that the Rebel cause drew a well-qualified corps of military leaders, equal to 30 percent of the U.S. Army's officer staff before the war began. The Confederate War Office was skilled at spreading these highly talented men across the South to mobile regional departments where they would lead and train inexperienced volunteers for the war. The Confederate Army was consistently able to ready itself for battle twice as fast as the North. Over the long run, however, this did not override the fact that the Federals were able to raise three times as many men in their army throughout the war.

This ability to put men in the field much quicker than the North gave the South an advantage early in the war that helped produce early field victories, extending the war. This, too, in a way, was an advantage for the South. The longer the Rebel armies could stretch out the war, the more restless Northern civilians became about the conflict that did not seem to have an immediate end. That advantage was two-edged, however, for the longer the war continued, the wider the gap in the South's ability to supply its men.

As to putting men into uniform and delivering them to the battlefield, both sides performed Herculean efforts during the first year of the conflict. Union forces had numbered about 16,000 men at the opening of the conflict in the spring of 1861. By midsummer, the North had increased its military numbers by more than ten times over, at about 186,000 men. Many men volunteered at the opening of hostilities, certain the war would be short and easily won. Some even feared the war might end before they could make it to enlist.

After a year of fighting, the rate of enlistment into the Union Army fell off dramatically, due to the realities of the conflict and its bloodletting. By July 1862, the U.S. Congress passed the Militia Act, which put in place the first military draft in U.S. history. President Lincoln supported the draft and called for an army of 600,000 men to enlist for nine months. By the end of 1862, the draft had created a Federal force more than three times its original size.

As for the Confederate Army, it started at zero, since it did not exist prior to early 1861, and reached 112,000 in number by mid-1861. Many of those signed on for a one-year enlistment, although many in the spring of 1861, like their Northern counterparts, did not expect the war to even last that long. Just as in the North, when those enlistments ran out in 1862, Confederate numbers began to dwindle. This led the Southern Congress to also start a draft. One difference between the two draft systems was obvious. Since the South had fewer men to rely on to fill its military ranks, Rebel draftees were signed on for three-year enlistments instead of a single year.

In that first year of fighting, the war produced an endless string of battles, both large and small in scale. Historians count 156 battles that took place during 1861 alone. In the total run of the war, this represented only 7 percent of the battle total. By 1862, the number of battles for the year shot up to 564, which translates into three battles every two days. By the end of 1862, the armies of the North and South had engaged in one-third of the battles fought during the entire war. Of those battles fought during 1861 and 1862, three-fifths were fought in the upper South, concentrated in Virginia, Tennessee, Missouri, and (technically neutral) Kentucky. These first two years of fighting introduced Northerners and Southerners alike to the carnage and hideous losses of a conflict whose end, by the end of 1862, was nowhere in sight.

commander of all Federal forces in the state, General David E. Twiggs, immediately surrendered in the name of all U.S. Army troops, about 4,000 men. This included Lee, who was still in command of the Department of Texas. Twiggs resigned his commission and joined the Confederacy. Lee left the West for the last time in his life and returned to Virginia, where he was assigned to command the 1st Regiment of Cavalry in March. President Lincoln, newly sworn in, signed Lee's papers.

Colonel Lee wrote letters mocking his fellow Southerners for their secessionist ways. Abandoning the Union, he believed, was a betrayal of the founding fathers. But Lee's opinions were pushed to the wall when, as the ghost of war loomed, Lee's old commander General Winfield Scott approached him about serving as his second in command in the event of war. Lee said he would consider the appointment, but only if his native Virginia did not opt to secede. When asked if he would ever fight for the newly forming Confederacy, Lee was clear concerning his ultimate loyalties, as noted by historian Freeman in *R.E. Lee*: "I shall never bear arms against the Union, but it may be necessary for me to carry a musket in the defense of my native state, Virginia, in which case I shall not prove recreant to my duty." Lee was opposed to the Confederacy, to secession, to separatism, and even to the institution of slavery, but, should his home state leave the Union, Lee's loyalties left him no choice: He would never be able to fight against Virginia.

Virginia did not secede before the fighting began. Those supporting secession held back until the opening of actual hostilities. War between the North and South opened following an attack on April 12 by Confederate gun batteries against Fort Sumter in Charleston Harbor. Five days later, Virginians attending a state convention voted to leave the Union, and Lee's decision concerning his future was cast. By April 20, he resigned his longtime commission with the U.S. Army, following his conscience. In words noted by historian Charles P. Roland, Lee stated: "I cannot raise my hand against my birthplace, my home, my children." It would be a fateful decision for Lee. When General Scott was handed Lee's resignation, he knew he had lost his best possible military advisor and general. According to historian Douglas Freeman, Scott told his former favorite: "Lee, you have made the greatest mistake of your life; but I feared it would be so."

JOINING THE CONFEDERACY

Lee's first duty as a comrade of the Confederacy was to accept an offer of command from Virginia governor John Letchner. The governor asked his fellow Virginian to command the state's militia forces. Little time passed before Confederate president Jefferson Davis came calling, asking Lee to become a part of the regular Confederate Army. Lee accepted the rank of brigadier general, a low position among generals. By mid-summer, however, Lee received his full generalship.

Throughout the first year of the Civil War, Robert E. Lee's legacy would have to wait. He was pressed into duty as he had been originally trained, as an engineer, not a field commander. When the first major battle of the war was fought in Virginia— it would later be known as First Bull Run or First Manassas (July 1861)—Lee was not present on the battlefield. Lee would write to his wife after the battle, according to historian Clifford Dowdey, telling her: "I wished to partake in the . . . struggle, and am mortified at my absence . . . But the President thought it more important that I should be here [in Richmond]. I could not have done as well as has been done, but I could have helped, and taken part in the struggle for my home and neighborhood." Lee finally did wrangle a field command out of President Davis that fall, but he was soon roundly defeated in western Virginia during the Battle of Cheat Mountain (September 10 to 14).

Davis called Lee back to Richmond following the loss and sent him off instead to South Carolina, Georgia, and Florida to carry out primarily supervisory military tasks. Lee had always been brilliant at designing fortifications, and his work through-out 1861 gained him the mocking label of the "King of Spades." Few could have known at the time that the Confederacy and President Davis were wasting Lee's true military talents.

Even though the war was only six months old, Lee was beginning to feel its effects. The 54-year-old military veteran's beard turned completely white.

Lee's contribution to the war changed by early summer of 1862. That May and June, Union commander George B. McClellan delivered more than 100,000 men on a peninsula lying between the York and James rivers and pointed them straight west, toward the heart of the Confederacy: Richmond. During the Battle of Seven Pines, Lee's future changed course. The commander of Confederate forces east of Richmond, Lee's old West Point comrade Joseph Johnston, was severely wounded. Johnston would have to surrender command, and he would take two years to fully recover. President Davis then turned to Lee to take command, which Lee accepted on June 1, 1862.

Lee still had his personal doubts about his professional abilities as a military commander. According to historian Sobel, Lee later reflected: "I wish that [Johnston's] mantle had fallen upon an abler man." As for Johnston, according to historian Earle Rice, he held Lee in great confidence: "The shot that struck me down is the best that has been fired for the Southern cause yet, for I possess in no degree the confidence of our govern-ment, and now they have in place one who does." For nearly three years, until the end of the war, General Robert E. Lee re-mained the commander of Rebel forces he would call the Army of Northern Virginia.

A LEGACY AS COMMANDER

Seemingly countless books have been written describing Rob-ert E. Lee's command of the Army of Northern Virginia. Few historians consider him to be anything less than the greatest

Leading up to the Battle of Chancellorsville (above), Union general Joseph "Fighting Joe" Hooker bragged that he and the Army of the Potomac were prepared to defeat General Robert E. Lee and the Rebels. Claiming that his military plans were perfect, Hooker went on to say, " May God have mercy on General Lee, for I will have none." When the conflict ended, the Union was soundly defeated and the Battle of Chancellorsville became known as Lee's greatest victory.

general of the war. During his three years as commander, he led an army that would see incredible carnage and fight in some of the hardest fought engagements of the war. He would prove himself the South's best hope for victory almost immediately after taking command. Within weeks of the Seven Pines engagement, Lee fought McClellan to a standstill during a week of fighting known as the Seven Days (June 25 to July 1). The week ended with the Union commander evacuating his positions on the Virginia peninsula and returning to the relative safety of Washington, D.C.

Over the next six months, Lee engaged Union forces in three major battles: Second Bull Run, Antietam, and Fredericksburg. By the spring of 1863, he defeated another Union commander, General Joseph Hooker, in a brilliantly fought battle at Chancellorsville, Virginia. On every occasion, Lee maneuvered, planned, and fought better than his opponent. One of Lee's great skills was that he selected the best military commanders. After taking command, Lee cleaned house within the ranks of Johnston's former staff. He eliminated those officers whose skills he doubted. He also chose two generals he felt he could rely on to take command of forces he would use as his two flanks. One was 41-year-old General James Longstreet, whom soldiers referred to as "Old Pete." The other was Thomas "Stonewall" Jackson. These two commanders—Longstreet and Jackson—would play crucial roles in battles over the following year.

FOUGHT TO A STANDSTILL

Following Lee's smashing victory against General Hooker at Chancellorsville in the spring of 1862, his fortunes of war began to take a turn. During the first three days of July, he engaged the Union Army at a sleepy Pennsylvania crossroads called Gettysburg. There, he miscalculated against a new commander of the Army of the Potomac, General George G. Meade. Lee had not planned on fighting at Gettysburg, but, once his advance guard accidentally smashed into the Union advance, the battle was on. Lee could have chosen to pull back, allow the Federals to give him chase, and select a different field on which to fight, one offering him better field position and the high ground (which his troops failed to secure on the first day of fighting). But he chose not to, deciding he would engage the enemy. Historian Bevin Alexander recalled Lee's words after his second in command, General James Longstreet, tried to talk him out of fighting at Gettysburg. "The enemy is there, and I am going to attack him there," Lee stated. "They are there in position, and I am going to whip them or they are going to whip me."

Lee's decision to fight at Gettysburg turned out to be a disaster, with his army experiencing 28,000 casualties, losses it could not afford. This loss placed Lee in a difficult position to fight throughout the remainder of 1863. By the spring of 1864, he was facing a Union general who had accomplished a sterling military record of wins on the battlefield in the western theater—Ulysses S. Grant—whom Lincoln transferred to direct the Army of the Potomac. Through nearly two months of fighting across the Virginia landscape, with Grant moving constantly by his left flank closer and closer to Richmond, the two armies battered one another bloody, with both sides taking extraordinary losses.

Finally, by June 1864, Grant had bottled up Lee in Petersburg, south of Richmond, with no means of escape without leaving Richmond vulnerable to Union attack. For the remainder of the war, Lee was trapped. By the spring of 1865, he and his men could hold out no longer. He ordered them to break out of Petersburg and make a run to the west, hoping to join up with another Rebel army under the command of General Joe Johnston. But within days, Grant's army caught up with Lee's at Appomattox Court House, where the Southern general surrendered, effectively ending the war.

AFTERMATH OF WAR

With the Civil War ended, Robert E. Lee was a man without an army or even a country. Although some Northerners wanted to try him as a traitor for having taken up arms against the United

States, most Americans were not prepared to place Lee on trial and he was granted amnesty.

Lee did not live long to see the new South take root—a South without slavery, a region defeated and destroyed by war. During the five years following the nightmare conflict, Lee served, not as a military commander, but as an educator. In 1865, he accepted the presidency of a small academic institution, Washington College in Lexington, Virginia. He increased the enrollment of the college during his time there and became a respected leader on campus. He died in 1870 at age 63, having spent years not only personally encouraging his students at Washington College, but also his fellow Southerners as a whole against holding onto any bitterness about the war.

Robert E. Lee had led the Army of Northern Virginia through great victories against larger numbers of Union men at each engagement. He had proven himself a genius at prolonging the war, or avoiding capture by superior numbers of the enemy, and of winning battles other generals might have easily lost. Lee had fought without any expectation that the South would ultimately win the conflict. Although he had not supported secession against the United States prior to the war, he still considered himself honor-bound to fight for his native state. Through Lee's efforts, successes, and unique leadership, the Southern war effort became the stuff of legend.

Ulysses S. Grant

Future U.S. president Ulysses S. Grant was born in a log cabin, just as his two predecessors, Abraham Lincoln and Andrew Johnson, had been. He was born a Northerner; his mother, Hannah Simpson Grant, delivered him on April 27, 1822, in Point Pleasant, Ohio. He was the first of six children born to Hannah and her husband, Jesse Root Grant. The Grant family came from English immigrant stock. Jesse Grant had lived his earlier years in Pennsylvania and earned his livelihood as a tanner. It was in Pennsylvania that he had met his future bride, a resident of Horsham Township.

RAISED A WESTERNER

Before Ulysses turned two years old, his family moved to Georgetown, Ohio, where his father continued to work as a tanner, as well as a farmer. It was while they lived at George-town that Ulysses's five siblings were born. Through the years of Ulysses's childhood, his father prospered as a tanner. When his son became old enough, Jesse pulled him into the business to teach him the trade. But young Ulysses did not enjoy the tanning yard with its bad odors and chemicals. The sight of blood made him nauseous, a problem he had all his life. (As an adult, even a trace of blood from meat on his plate made his sick.) He did enjoy working the family farm, however, especially working with horses. By his teen years, he had become an excellent horseman. His love of horses would continue throughout his life. Although the tanning business was not for him, Ulysses gained a solid work ethic and could be trusted with tasks assigned to him.

Ulysses attended school in Georgetown through age 14. Then, he was sent to a school in Maysville, Kentucky, across the Ohio River. After a year, he was sent to a private academy in the neighboring town of Ripley, Ohio. The following year, when Ulysses was 17, he was accepted into West Point.

Academy life for Ulysses Grant was a mixed experience. He was not an exceptional student by any means, except in the field of mathematics, in which he excelled. He also proved himself well-suited in horsemanship. As for many of his other studies, he did well enough but not exceptionally well. He spent too much time reading fiction, including adventures and other novels, and not enough time on his academic studies. The longer Grant remained at West Point, the more he was certain that army life was not for him. He was soon biding his time, hoping to ride out his four years at the academy and then take his newly developed skills into the civilian workforce and find a good job. At one point, he considered becoming a college mathematics professor.

THE ARMY LIFE

Grant graduated from West Point in 1843, ranked 21st out of 39 graduating cadets, gaining a commission as a second lieutenant. Despite his horse skills, Grant was not given a cavalry posting; such postings were popular and chosen by classmates with

Originally named Hiram Ulysses Grant, the future Union general changed his name when he enrolled in the United States Military Academy at West Point. Grant, showing only an aptitude for math and riding, remained undistinguished until he served under generals Zachary Taylor and Winfield Scott in the Mexican-American War.

higher academic rankings than Grant. He was instead assigned as a regimental quartermaster, which made him responsible for supplies and equipment. Despite his earlier plans to leave military service, Grant took a posting at St. Louis with the 4th Infantry Regiment. It was during his post in St. Louis that Grant met the young woman he would one day marry. Julia Dent was a local girl, the sister of a fellow cadet at West Point. Through the following years, the Grants would have four children, three boys and a girl.

Grant had just been out of West Point and assigned to St. Louis when rumors began to circulate that the United States and Mexico would soon be at war with one another. For a while, such rumors even managed to postpone his wedding. The dispute between the United States and Mexico centered on the alleged boundary between the two countries. Mexico claimed the border lay along the banks of the Nueces River, while the U.S. government argued the border was actually along the Rio Grande. After several years of blustering between the two countries, war finally broke out in 1846.

By 1844, Grant's regiment had been assigned to a facility in Louisiana, followed by a move to Texas the following year. Stationed in Texas, Grant soon found himself assigned to territory claimed by Mexico. Grant's regiment participated in the war, and he served through most of the conflict as his regiment's quartermaster. However, he was not always a behind-the-scenes commander. On several occasions, he led his company into the direct fighting while under the command of General Zachary Taylor, who would be elected U.S. president in 1848.

During the Mexican-American War, Grant's regiment was transferred under the direct command of General Winfield Scott, who operated during the early months of the short war along the West Coast. Grant personally saw action at Monterrey, where he once volunteered to deliver a field message to another U.S. officer, which required him to make his way through the town's streets on horseback under heavy sniper fire. He also participated in the fighting during the battles of Resaca de la Palma and Palo Alto. He gained brevets (temporary rank promotions granted in the field) for his efforts during the fighting at Molino del Rey and at Chapultepec, during the U.S. Army overland campaign to capture Mexico City.

During one battle, Grant spotted his future brother-in-law Fred Dent lying on the battlefield, having taken a serious wound in the leg. Grant ran forward under fire and rescued him. While Grant was helping Dent to safety, a Mexican soldier came forward, intent on sneaking up behind them. Fortunately, a fellow soldier shot and killed the enemy. When U.S. forces reached the Mexican capital, Grant was there, again a witness to the action. He was later praised for his participation in the battle and was promoted for his personal bravery. By the end of 1847, he had achieved the rank of first lieutenant. After the conflict was over and the U.S. Army was victorious, Grant's regiment was temporarily assigned to remain in Mexico City.

Writing nearly 40 years later, Grant criticized the United States's involvement in the Mexican-American War. In his memoirs, which he penned just before his death in 1885, Grant referred to the war as a mistake, an unjust action taken by the more powerful United States. He said the war had been brought on by Southerners who wanted to defeat Mexico so they could gain new territory and expand slavery into the Southwest. His feelings about the war were made clear, when he wrote: "I was bitterly opposed to the measure (the war itself) and to this day, regard the war, which resulted, as one of the most unjust ever waged by a stronger against a weaker nation." Despite his negative opinion of the United States's reasons for going to war with Mexico, his war experiences helped form him as a military man. During the war, he had many opportunities to watch superior officers making decisions, and the lessons were not lost on him.

After spending some additional months in Mexico, Grant returned to St. Louis to marry Julia Dent. Their wedding took place on August 22, 1848. Grant's marriage to Julia proved one of the greatest positives throughout his entire life. The two were immensely devoted to one another and remained deeply in love. Julia would remain one of Grant's most constant encouragements.

Even with his war experiences behind him, he did not take advantage of his circumstances and resign his commission. He and his regiment were assigned to new posts farther east, including Detroit, followed by Sackets Harbor, New York. Grant's regiment was also assigned to several different postings on the West Coast. By 1852, the 4th Infantry Regiment was sent to Fort Vancouver in the Washington Territory. Grant and Julia had been married for several years, and at that time she was eight months pregnant with their second child. Despite his officer's rank, Grant did not make enough money to be able to afford to move his family out to the Pacific Northwest, and the army would not pay for such family moves, so he was often separated from his wife and children. Grant was a family man, and such separation proved emotionally difficult for him. In the meantime, Julia and their son, Frederick Dent Grant, went to live with Jesse and Hannah Grant back in Ohio.

Grant's posting at Fort Vancouver proved extremely difficult for him. He was often lonely and even bored, and he began to suffer from depression. It was at Vancouver that Grant appears to have turned to alcohol too often. How much Grant drank and how often is a subject of dispute among historians. It appears he was not a man who drank often under normal circumstances, but one who drank when he was feeling low and lonely, which Grant often was while separated from his family. Nevertheless, his drinking appears to have become a problem. Gossip began to circulate about it.

In 1854, Grant experienced some positive changes. He was promoted to full captain (at the time, the U.S. Army had only 50 captains in its ranks) and he was assigned to a new post, this time at Fort Humboldt in California. But the same problems remained. He still could not afford to move his family to the fort, so he remained lonely. As a result, his drinking continued, and the problem finally came to a head. By the summer of 1854, Grant abruptly resigned his commission and returned to civilian life. Rumors suggested that his commanding officer, Brevet Lieutenant Colonel Robert C. Buchanan, discovered Grant drunk while on duty as a pay officer.

The story goes that Buchanan offered Grant two choices. He could either resign from the army or face possible expulsion through court martial. With only poor choices available, Grant chose to leave military service. Historians are uncertain of the truth. An equally likely story presumes that Grant, tired of being separated from his family, chose to leave of his own free will. There is no real proof that the Buchanan story is true. As for Grant's military record, the U.S. Department of War claimed at the time, according to historian William McFeely: "Nothing stands against [Grant's] good name."

A CIVILIAN ONCE MORE

At age 32, Grant returned to St. Louis and was reunited with his family. But Grant's return to civilian life would be filled with ups and downs. The six years following his resignation from military service were filled with constant failures and financial worries. Julia's father gave her a piece of land outside St. Louis for the Grants to farm. Grant built a cabin on the property, which he called Hardscrabble, and worked the land for the next three years, until 1858. Although Grant liked farming in general, he found it difficult to make ends meet, given poor farm prices. In 1857, the entire country fell into an economic depression, which hit Grant and his family hard. He sometimes cut and sold firewood to help make some extra money.

On the farm, Grant sometimes used slaves for labor, most of whom were owned by his father. During these years, Grant himself owned a single slave, whom he decided to free in 1859. Julia owned four slaves—two female domestic slaves and their two young boys.

By 1859, after struggling with his unsuccessful farm, Grant sold the land and moved into St. Louis with his family. Life in the Missouri river town was not much better than it had been on the farm. He struggled to find a job. For a while, he worked in a relative's real estate office, collecting rents, but he hated the work and was poor at it. He then got a government job in the U.S. Customs House, a political appointment.

Grant was not, by nature, a political creature. He was not outspoken concerning politics, even though his father-in-law was a Democrat. He did not hold the U.S. Customs House job as county engineer for long. It appears his father-in-law's Democratic leanings lost his son-in-law his employment.

Things went from bad to worse. Grant was forced to ask his own father for a job and, by 1860, was employed in Grant & Perkins, a leather goods and supply store in Galena, Illinois. The shop mainly sold saddles and harnesses. To make circumstances worse, Grant was employed as an assistant to his two younger brothers, who had stuck with the family business. But at least Grant was working on the retail side of the tanning business. He was paid $50 a month but had little skill as a storekeeper. All in all, these were difficult times filled with frustrations and failures that gave no hint of the status Grant would soon gain in his life due to war and politics.

A RETURN TO MILITARY SERVICE

The year 1860 ushered in a series of events that brought permanent redirection to the life of Ulysses S. Grant. Since leaving military service six years earlier, he had proved himself lackluster in almost every endeavor. Few who knew him thought Grant was destined for anything important in life, much less fame and a national reputation that would one day catapult him to the U.S. presidency.

The 1860 election was controversial, its outcome threatening to signal whether or not a divided nation would plunge into secession and war. That year, Grant did not even bother to vote. Abraham Lincoln won the election, angering an already disgruntled South that feared the Illinois Republican was a secret abolitionist determined to destroy slavery. Beginning in December, Southern states began to secede and establish their own country to protect their way of life. With the country unraveling, war soon followed as Confederate artillery batteries surrounding Charleston Harbor bombarded federal Fort Sumter in April 1861. War had come.

Although Grant had hung up his uniform seven years earlier, he had little to show for those hard, frustrating years. He was only 39 years old, and the country was looking for military leaders. Grant soon saw the handwriting on the wall. Although not loudly political, he was opposed to secession and was ready to fight to restore his country. When President Lincoln, newly sworn into office in early March, called for 75,000 volunteers for military service, Grant knew what he had to do. His country would need experienced military veterans and especially officers who were West Point grads.

Immediately, he formed a volunteer company in Galena. He then took a trip to the Illinois state capital in Springfield where he served under the state's adjutant general. Grant soon requested a colonel's commission from the federal government, but his request was turned down. In June 1861, Illinois governor Richard Yates appointed him colonel over a regiment of state volunteers, the Illinois 21st.

Even though Grant was now commanding Illinois men, his first task was to take them into Missouri where they were to protect the Hannibal and St. Joseph Railroad. Missouri was a border state, a slave state that had not yet seceded, so its future was uncertain. The state's governor, Claiborne Jackson, was pro-Confederate, even though he announced Missouri would be armed and neutral, ready to fight troops from either side that entered the state.

By August, the state was in Union hands and Governor Jackson was removed from office. That same month, Grant received his federal commission. Illinois congressman Elihu B. Washburne had made the request on Grant's behalf directly to President Lincoln, who gave Grant the rank of brigadier general. Before month's end, the western theater commander,

Grant and the Presidency

Ulysses S. Grant is remembered in the pages of history not only for leading the Union to ultimate victory over the Confederates during the Civil War, but for another accomplishment: serving as the nation's eighteenth president. He was elected to two terms and held the office from 1869 until 1877. The Grant presidency was a complicated one. He was not a politician or civil leader by nature, and several members of his administration were openly engaging in fraud and other offenses. The Grant years became known for their corruption, although Grant himself was not involved in such scandalous behaviors.

Grant was in office during the last half of Reconstruction, the period between 1865 and 1877 when the federal government worked to rebuild the South in the aftermath of the Civil War. During those years, federal officials forced changes to the Constitution that allowed blacks to receive their citizenship and to vote. Generally, Grant supported these moves. Throughout his presidency he remained relatively committed to the establishment and protection of black civil rights.

Major General John C. Fremont, appointed Grant to command the District of Southeast Missouri. After seven years of failure, Grant was finding his way back.

"UNCONDITIONAL SURRENDER"

At last his West Point training was paying off again, and Grant was finding a place for himself in the officer ranks of the U.S. Army. Slowly, methodically, he was in command of men during wartime and began to show others the leadership qualities he

After his presidency, Grant went on a two-year world tour with his wife, Julia. He was well received by various heads of state, including Queen Victoria of England and Prince Bismarck of Germany. His travels took him from Europe to the Middle East to Asia. By 1879, a faction of the Republican Party was willing to support Grant for a third term as president, but the move ultimately failed. In 1881, Grant experienced financial troubles when he invested in a banking partnership with Ferdinand Ward, who ultimately cheated Grant and other investors, leaving the former president on the verge of bankruptcy. The year was 1884, and Grant soon received a second dose of bad news when he was diagnosed with throat cancer.

Since U.S. presidents at that time were not provided with pensions, he needed to make money as quickly as possible to provide for his family after his death. The famous American writer Mark Twain approached him and offered to publish the former general's memoirs. Grant struggled through his final months writing his autobiography, finishing his work just prior to his death. Grant's memoirs were widely popular, selling 300,000 copies and earning his family royalties of nearly a half million dollars. At his death, Grant was 63. He lies buried today in New York City's Riverside Park.

Upon Grant's resignation from the military in 1854, his father-in-law purchased a plot of land for the returning war hero to build a farm. Grant built a cabin and called the home Hardscrabble (above), but he soon sold the property when farming could not provide for his family. Grant was not particularly good at anything, and he struggled to find an appropriate occupation until he was called to serve in the Civil War.

possessed. He did not wait for the battle to find him. He had no intentions of sitting through the conflict in an office. He wanted to see the war, wanted to make a difference.

And he did not have to wait long. By September, he was on his way to Kentucky to secure the river town of Paducah, which stood where the Tennessee and Ohio rivers joined. In fact, he beat the Confederates into the town, as they had determined

Paducah's strategic location, as well. (Although Kentucky, another border state, had declared its neutrality, Rebel troops had entered it anyway.) Then, in November, Grant saw his first battle of the war, even if it was only a small engagement. He met Confederate troops at Belmont, Missouri, but the action there decided nothing, as Grant drove them out of town, only to have Confederate units return and reoccupy their positions.

Then, three months later, General Grant saw his first major action of the war, for which he would gain national notice. While most other armies remained immobile during the winter months, Grant chose to move on two Confederate military targets: Fort Donelson on the Cumberland River and Fort Henry on the Tennessee River. The two forts were only 12 miles (19 km) apart, at locations where the two rivers flowed close to one another. Fort Henry fell easily, with help from Union gunboats, as it was partially flooded by recent rains. The Confederates there retreated to Fort Donelson. There, Grant's army was surprise attacked by the same Rebel commander he'd met at Belmont, Brigadier General Gideon J. Pillow.

When the attack began, Grant was not present with his forces. But he arrived on the scene and systemically, even coolly, reorganized his men and mounted a successful counterattack. Then the general ordered a siege of the fort. Meanwhile, the two superior Confederate officers evacuated the fort, leaving Brigadier General Simon Buckner in command. When he asked Grant for terms of surrender, the Union commander stood his ground, announcing, according to historian Geoffrey Ward, "No terms except an unconditional and immediate surrender can be accepted." Buckner soon surrendered the fort's garrison of 12,000 men. From that time on, U.S. Grant became "Unconditional Surrender" Grant.

At a time when the Union cause needed a victory in the field, Grant became an overnight success. The fall of Fort Henry and Fort Donelson amounted to the North's first two significant victories of the war. When a newspaperman wrote that

Grant was a smoker (of pipes, since he had never been able to afford cigars), the public began sending him cigars by the barrel. Smoking cigars became a lifelong habit, and he even claimed after the war that he smoked 10,000 cigars in five years. Unfortunately, he would die of mouth and throat cancer 20 years after the war.

SHILOH AND VICKSBURG

Ironically, Grant's success in the field made him the target of jealousy on the part of his superior, Major General Henry W. Halleck. Believing Grant to be a drunk and accusing him of ignoring the chain of command, Halleck relieved Grant of his field command. However, President Lincoln, believing Grant to represent the Union's best hope in the western theater, personally stepped in and forced Halleck to restore Grant to his former command just two weeks later. Grant's new command, in fact, was even more significant. He was to lead the newly formed Army of the Tennessee.

Grant had been restored for only a few weeks before he engaged his army in the largest field battle in the western theater to that date in the war. The Battle of Shiloh opened on April 6, 1862, in southwest Tennessee, pitting Grant against one of the South's most capable generals, Albert Sidney Johnston. The battle began when Confederate troops surprised Grant's men at Pittsburg Landing, with the Union men barely managing to hold back a complete battering by the enemy through the first day of fighting. (Grant and his men did not realize that General Johnston had been killed during the battle.) With their backs to the Tennessee River, Grant and his troops appeared trapped and prime for the Confederates to defeat on a second day of fighting. However, the Federal forces were reinforced overnight by the arrival of 25,000 fresh troops who arrived by steamboat, accompanied by Union gunboats.

Grant won the battle, having managed to keep his control of the field and by refusing to panic in the face of hard fighting by his Southern opponents. The battle was costly, however, and critics charged Grant with having lost thousands of men. But, again, Lincoln supported his western commander, stating, as noted by historian Geoffrey Ward, "I can't spare this man—he fights!"

Once again, a Grant victory had not come cheap. At that date, it was the bloodiest battle of the war, with more than 23,000 casualties. Again, Halleck stepped in, taking personal command of Grant's army, while reducing Grant to serve directly under him. Grant was so dissatisfied and frustrated by Halleck's treatment that he considered leaving the army altogether, but his friend in arms, General William Tecumseh Sherman, convinced him to reconsider. By mid-summer, Grant's direct dilemma was solved when Halleck was promoted and called to the Department of War in Washington, D.C. Grant received his former command and right away won small-scale battles in Tennessee at Corinth and Iuka.

Grant remained a relentless commander as the war continued through 1862 and into 1863. During much of the year following his victory at Shiloh, the western commander remained preoccupied with an extended, complicated, and sometimes frustrated campaign to bring about the fall of Vicksburg, Mississippi, then the last major Southern holdout along the Mississippi River. His strategy would prove to be an elongated masterpiece. Even during the winter of 1862 to 1863, Grant and his men remained on the move, trying to find a way to approach Vicksburg by land. By the late spring of 1863, Grant had captured Jackson, the Mississippi capital located east of Vicksburg, and marched his men against the last holdout Confederate force protecting the river city. After laying a siege of six weeks, Vicksburg finally fell into Grant's hands on July 4, 1863.

THE PRESIDENT'S MAN

The success of Grant in the western theater was even more significant at the time, when compared to the lack of success in the eastern theater on the part of the main Union force, the Army of the Potomac. The Union forces in Virginia were fighting under various unsuccessful commanders, such as George B. McClellan, or overall hopeless ones, such as John Pope and Ambrose Burnside. These Federals were fighting the Army of Northern Virginia, led by the South's brilliant General Robert E. Lee. Pope and Burnside were fighting hard but losing almost constantly.

Following Grant's victory at Shiloh, McClellan lost his campaign on the Virginia peninsula against Lee. As Grant won at Corinth, Pope lost to Lee at Second Bull Run. Although McClellan managed to fight Lee to a standstill at Antietam in September, the Army of the Potomac lost dramatically less than three months later in a disastrous fight at Fredericksburg. In the spring of 1863, Lee defeated Union forces at Chancellorsville, while Grant won at Jackson and successfully brought about the fall of Vicksburg. That victory, plus a win at Gettysburg (July 1 to 3) by General Meade, the latest commander of the Army of the Potomac, proved the turning point of the war. Lincoln was so pleased with Grant by the summer of 1863, according to historian Geoffrey Ward, that the president declared: "Grant is my man and I am his the rest of the war."

Lincoln made good on his confidence in Grant. By October 1863, he placed Grant in command of the Military Division of Mississippi. At that time, a Federal army had become bottled up in Chattanooga, Tennessee, where Confederate forces were laying siege, threatening to starve out the Union men. Lincoln sent Grant to Chattanooga to rescue the failed Northern commander, General William Rosecrans, and his army. Grant helped to turn the tide against the Confederates. He ordered a multipronged attack against Rebel entrenchments on Lookout Mountain, which towers above Chattanooga, as well as Missionary Ridge. On November 25, the Union men broke the Southern positions and Grant was credited with yet another victory in the field.

His efforts again inspired President Lincoln, who advanced Grant to the rank of lieutenant general in the regular army. No one since George Washington (with the exception of General Winfield Scott's brevet appointment during the Mexican-American War) had ever held that high of a rank. In fact, Congress had to pass a special bill restoring the rank on March 2, 1864, with Grant receiving his new rank less than two weeks later. For Grant, his prewar failures at shopkeeping and bill collecting seemed far in the past.

By the spring of 1864, Grant faced his most capable opponent of the war. With the Army of the Potomac in Virginia having experienced a string of commanders, most of whom Lee had defeated, Lincoln appointed Grant to fight in Virginia for the first time since the opening of the war. Perhaps Grant could bring some of his success to the fight against the South's most victorious commander. From early May through June, Grant led his men through a nonstop series of brutal battles, all designed to bring the Army of Northern Virginia to its knees. Unlike previous commanders in the East who typically fought a battle against Lee, retreated, and then laid low during months of inactivity and recovery until the next battle, Grant fought a string of engagements and refused to back off of his goal: to defeat Robert E. Lee ultimately for the purpose of ending the war once and for all.

From the Battle of the Wilderness to Spotsylvania to North Anna to the bloody Cold Harbor fight, Grant continued to pound at Lee's army, all the while moving his men by the left flank in a swinging arc toward Richmond. Two days of fighting in the Wilderness outside Chancellorsville resulted in thousands of casualties and no clear advantage for either side. The Battle of Spotsylvania Court House dragged on for two weeks.

In the midst of this long fight, Grant expressed his intent and resolve, as noted by historian James McPherson, when he sent a message to Lincoln: "I propose to fight it out along this line if it takes all summer." The following day, May 12, Union

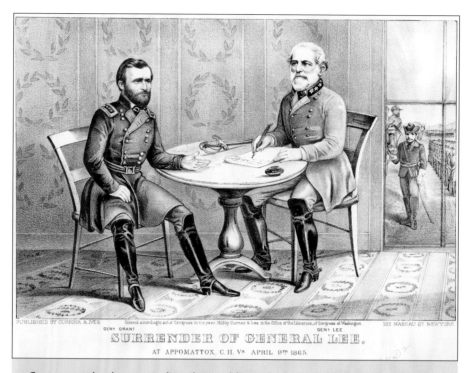

PUBLISHED BY CURRIER & IVES   Entered according to act of Congress in the year 1873 by Currier & Ives in the Office of the Librarian of Congress at Washington.   185 NASSAU ST NEW YORK.

GEN⁺ GRANT   GEN⁺ LEE

SURRENDER OF GENERAL LEE.

AT APPOMATTOX, C. H. Vᴬ APRIL 9ᵀᴴ 1865.

Grant proved to be extraordinarily capable on the battlefield during the Civil War. Under his leadership, the Union was able to secure crucial victories against General Robert E. Lee's Confederate Army. Refusing to accept anything less than "unconditional and immediate surrender" from his enemies, Grant was able to secure the official terms of surrender from Lee at Appomattox Court House in Virginia (above).

forces broke Lee's line and captured 4,000 Rebels. Casualties ran extremely high, and Grant was again criticized for his seemingly careless regard for the lives of his troops. But he had long come to understand that, to defeat the South, he and the entire Union Army would have to engage in total war: the absolute destruction of the South's armies, its population, its cities, and its ability to prolong the war. Grant's overall strategy saw success. By late June, he had fought Lee to the gates of Petersburg, south of Richmond, where the Union commander soon laid down a siege, bottling Lee and his men in and around the key railroad town. That siege would continue for the next nine months, keeping Lee from fighting effectively until the end of the war.

By April 1865, the end arrived for General Lee and his army. Reduced to a skeleton force, Lee tried to break out of Petersburg, leaving Richmond to be captured finally by Federal forces. Lee's army was soon surrounded in western Virginia and forced to surrender to General Grant on April 9.

Grant had proven himself a capable commander in the eastern theater and the most successful of the North's generals. He had constantly fought with bulldog determination and had kept his cool repeatedly even in the midst of battles that appeared on the edge of loss. He had developed a fighting style based on outmaneuvering the enemy. Rarely did he shy away from direct assaults, even when they delivered heavy casualties to his army. With each such engagement, Grant had understood that the outcome of the war was always about slowly wearing down Confederate forces until they had simply lost the will and ability to fight. Fortunately, Lincoln remained a supporter of Grant and refused to pull him from command. Grant may have lost battles during his fight against Lee in 1864, but he ultimately won his campaign and, in doing so, helped win the war.

Thomas "Stonewall" Jackson

Few Confederate generals are remembered today with greater awe and respect than the commander who served as Robert E. Lee's right-hand man in the field from the spring of 1862 through the year that followed. This man was General Thomas "Stonewall" Jackson. As daring and bold as Lee became throughout the war as the commander of the Army of Northern Virginia, Jackson too became known for his daring exploits, including his brilliant Shenandoah Valley campaign and as a corps commander under Lee.

Although Lee is remembered for his great masterpiece of battle—Chancellorsville, May 1863—his success was due, at least in dramatic part, to Jackson's successful expedition through nearly 15 miles (24 km) of woods thought to be impossible to navigate. This allowed Jackson to swing wide of Union forces for an entire day, only to surprise the Federals and smash Northern commander Joseph Hooker's right flank. Despite his contribution in adding that day to Lee's legacy as the war's greatest Southern general, Jackson's success that single day at Chancellorsville would prove his last. The loss of Stonewall Jackson that late spring, at the war's halfway mark, would prove to be one from which Lee would never recover.

Ultimately, Jackson is considered by modern historians to have been one of the most skilled and capable tactical commanders during the Civil War. His military campaigns and movements in the field are studied in military history classes and have become textbook lessons. His actions would be remembered as bold, determined, responsive, and innovative during the First Battle of Bull Run (it was there that Jackson gained the nickname "Stonewall"), Second Bull Run, the bloody single day of fighting at Antietam (Sharpsburg), Fredericksburg, and then, finally, at Chancellorsville. He did not always perform well in the field; for that matter, neither did Lee. His actions during the week of fighting known as the Seven Days, when Lee had just taken command of the Army of Northern Virginia, were weak, and he was slow in carrying out Lee's orders. His slowness is almost inexplicable even today.

But when he was killed at Chancellorsville, ironically by Confederate friendly fire, his failures seemed to matter little. Jackson lost an arm by amputation due to his wounds and lay dying. Lee sent his able lieutenant a personal message through a military chaplain. Historian James Robertson recalled Lee's affectionate words: "Give General Jackson my affectionate regards, and say to him: he has lost his left arm but I my right."

JACKSON'S EARLY YEARS

Despite his success as a commander of Southern forces during the Civil War, Stonewall Jackson's earlier life had not always been marked by such legendary military skills. Jackson's life began simply, with seemingly few advantages and even fewer prospects to leave a significant mark on U.S. history.

He was born on January 21, 1824, in frontier Clarksburg, Virginia (now West Virginia), to parents Jonathan Jackson and

Julia Beckwith Jackson. Jonathan and Julia were the third generation of the Jackson family to live in the United States. Thomas Jackson's great-grandfather, an Irishman named Thomas Jonathan Jackson, had moved to London as a young man, where he was found guilty of larceny (he had stolen £170). His sentence was to become an indentured servant to a landowner in the United States.

During his passage on a prison ship, the *Litchfield*, in May 1749, Thomas Jonathan met another petty thief, Elizabeth Neddles. She was a hearty blond woman who stood over 6 feet tall (1.8 m) and was a native of London who had also been convicted of stealing. (In her case, she had pilfered 19 silver pieces, several pieces of jewelry, and some lace.) She, too, had been sentenced to seven years as an indentured servant in colonial America. When the *Litchfield* docked in Annapolis, Maryland, the Irishman and the Englishwoman had fallen in love.

Although they soon departed and would serve their indentures working for different Maryland masters, they continued their relationship and married in the summer of 1755. Once they completed their services, the Jacksons moved west in search of farmland, settling in Moorefield, Virginia (now West Virginia), by 1758. Through the years, Thomas Jonathan and Elizabeth had several children, bought additional farm acreage by the thousands of acres, and became solid frontier citizens. When the Revolutionary War caught up to them in western Virginia, Thomas and his two teenaged sons joined the cause and engaged in the fighting at the Battle of Kings Mountain in October 1780. By war's end, Thomas was a captain. Thomas's second son, Edward Jackson, would become Stonewall Jackson's grandfather. His son Jonathan Jackson would be Stonewall's father.

Jonathan Jackson grew up to become an attorney and married Julia Beckwith, also a native of Virginia. Thomas J. Jackson was their third child, named after his mother's grandfather. While Thomas was a toddler, the family experienced

A soldier from humble beginnings, Stonewall Jackson managed to educate himself enough to earn a place at the U.S. Military Academy at West Point. Though unremarkable at first, Jackson's sheer grit and determination pushed his school ranking from the bottom of the class to seventeenth. Jackson graduated from West Point and fought with distinction in the Mexican-American War, a conflict that introduced him to his future commander, Robert E. Lee.

severe losses. Thomas's older sister died of typhoid fever during the spring of 1826, when Thomas was only two. Then, young Thomas's father caught the same disease and died less than three weeks later.

Just a day after Jonathan Jackson's death, the newly widowed Julia gave birth to a baby girl, Laura Ann. Suddenly, Julia Jackson was without a husband, with three young children to care for. Her husband had left her with such significant debts that she was forced to sell the family's belongings to cover them. Through the years that followed, Julia tried to make ends meet as best she could, taking in sewing and working as a schoolteacher. When family members tried to help her financially, she refused their charity. She and her three children lived in a small rented cottage.

Four years after her husband's death, Julia was remarried, to an attorney named Blake Woodson. But the marriage did not smooth the way for Julia or for her family. Woodson had no affection for his three stepchildren. There was so little love between stepfather and stepchildren that Woodson sent them to live with relatives, rather than allow them to remain in his house. Thomas Jackson and his sister, Laura Ann, went to live with an uncle, the owner of a gristmill in Lewis County in the farthest reaches of then western Virginia. Their older brother, Warren, was farmed out to other relatives.

Then, a year after her marriage, Julia became ill due to complications while giving birth. The three children (young Thomas nearly seven years old, while his brother was nine) were summoned back to their mother's side as her health worsened further until her death. Now, the three Jackson children had lost both their natural parents. Thomas and Laura Ann were soon sent back to Jackson's Mill, where they spent the next four years together.

Then, they were separated and sent to different relatives. Thomas was handed off to Isaac and Polly Brake. Polly was a sister to Thomas's father. The Brake farm was just a few miles outside Clarksburg. Again, young Thomas found himself in a household where he was not wanted. Isaac Brake proved so verbally abusive to Thomas that he ran away. Historian Robertson recalled how, when a cousin of Thomas's sent word to him, begging him to return to the Brake farm, 11-year-old Thomas refused, saying: "Maybe I ought to, ma'am, but I am not going to." Instead, he walked on his own nearly 20 miles (32 km) back to Jackson's Mill, where he found himself welcomed by several caring relatives. Until he turned 18, Jackson's Mill and its surroundings remained his home.

Through these years, Thomas Jackson lived on the farm of Cummins Jackson, one of his uncles. These were some of young Thomas's best years, even though he worked hard for his keep. Work on his uncle's farm included tending sheep and other livestock, as well as field labor on the annual wheat and corn harvests. There was so much work to be done that the youth's education was scattered at best. He attended school as he could and taught himself when he couldn't. He borrowed books and read from Cummins's small library. His uncle provided some of his education, since Cummins Jackson also worked as a schoolteacher.

Thomas became a teacher of sorts himself. One of his uncle's slaves asked Thomas to teach him to read, which he agreed to do, but only if the slave brought him pine knots (a joint of pine used for fuel) in exchange. Thomas would use the pine knots to provide light to read by, since he worked during days and had to reserve most of his reading time for after dark. Thomas held up his end of the bargain and taught the curious slave to read, even though it was against Virginia law to teach a black man, whether free or slave, to read. After becoming literate, the young slave ran away from Cummins Jackson, followed the Underground Railroad, and made his way to freedom in Canada. During Thomas's last years living

at Jackson's Mill, he followed in his uncle's footsteps and became a schoolteacher, too.

OFF TO MILITARY SCHOOL

In 1842, after growing up under difficult emotional circumstances, with both his natural parents having died, 18-year-old
Thomas J. Jackson took one of the greatest gambles of his life:
He applied for acceptance into the U.S. Military Academy at
West Point. There were immediate obstacles. His lack of formal
schooling was one, as he struggled with the entrance examina-
tions. Then, he did not receive a letter of acceptance. The honor
had gone instead to another capable young Virginian, selected
by his district's congressman. But when the new cadet reported
for duty at the prestigious academy, he remained only one day,
deciding the rigors of military training were not for him after
all. Jackson moved into the number one slot and replaced the
young man.

Once enrolled at West Point, as with young Jackson's other
life experiences, academy life was difficult. His shortcomings
in education were among the worst. Based on his examination
scores, Jackson entered his class ranked at the very bottom. He
was also nearly incapable of mingling socially with his classmates. Some said that he was so uncertain and shy that his fellow
cadets gave him no notice for the first six months of academy
training. Had they really taken notice, they might have found
Thomas Jackson to be quite the odd fellow, indeed.

Throughout his life, starting as a young man, Jackson held
several strange ideas about himself, along with many peculiar
practices. For one, he was a hypochondriac, always believing
himself to be ill in some way. He was always suffering from
some imagined ailment. Jackson even believed his alleged ill-
nesses were caused, in part, by his organs being arranged oddly
inside his body. He would never bend over because he was afraid

he might be pressing against something inside him that might not function properly if compressed. He would sit bolt upright, afraid he would squeeze his internal organs and throw his body out of balance. To restore that balance, he would stand for hours at a time with his right hand in the air.

Jackson worked extremely hard to overcome his shortfalls, electing to study almost constantly. Slowly, but steadily, with determination, the last-placed cadet worked his way each year upward in his ranking. By the time he graduated from West Point in 1846, he had moved up to 17th place out of 59 cadets, a true success. His fellow cadets had long ago finally taken notice of the disciplined Thomas Jackson. Some even claimed that, if the young Virginian from Jackson's Mill had had one more year to prove himself in the halls of the academy, he might have graduated at the top of his class. One of those who noticed Jackson's dogged struggle at West Point was upperclassman Ulysses S. Grant, whom Jackson would never engage in the field directly during the Civil War. Grant later recalled of Jackson, as noted by historian James Robertson: "He lived by his maxims."

Cadet Jackson, class of 1846, graduated just in time to engage in the Mexican-American War. He emerged from the academy with a brevet rank of second lieutenant in the 1st U.S. Artillery Regiment, and his unit served throughout the conflict in Mexico from 1846 until 1848. During his time in the field, Lieutenant Jackson participated in the siege of Veracruz, as well as the battles of Contreras and Chapultepec, and the march into Mexico City. It was during the war that Jackson had the opportunity to meet Robert E. Lee for the first time.

During his war service, Jackson became the center of controversy on more than one occasion. In the midst of the U.S. attack against the Mexican stronghold Chapultepec Castle, a superior gave him the order to pull his forces back from their position. Jackson disobeyed what he considered to be a "bad order," later explaining that, had he withdrawn from his location in the field, he would have put his men in more peril than they experienced by remaining in position, even though their artillery unit was outgunned by the enemy. In this case, his decision was proven correct. In fact, by holding his position, an infantry brigade had been able to move forward under the artillery cover provided by Jackson and his men.

Jackson later obeyed what he considered a "bad order," when he ordered his artillery to fire on a group of civilians in Mexico City after Mexican officials refused to surrender their capital after a U.S. deadline had come and gone. Both these episodes during Jackson's service during the Mexican-American War won him a field promotion to brevet rank of major.

SERVICE AFTER WAR

The Mexican-American War ended with a U.S. victory and new territory for the United States, including the region of the Southwest made up of California and modern-day Arizona and New Mexico. Jackson and his unit returned to the United States for peacetime duty, assigned to the Carlisle Barracks in Pennsylvania. His wartime service had been to Jackson's liking, but he found duty outside of war boring and unfulfilling. By 1851, Jackson resigned his commission, choosing to accept a teaching post at the Virginia Military Institute in Lexington. Soon, Jackson became a professor of natural and experimental philosophy and instructor of artillery tactics. In Jackson's day, "natural and experimental philosophy" was roughly the same as modern-day physics and included studies in such difficult subjects as astronomy, mechanics, acoustics, and optics.

Jackson's lessons are still part of the curriculum at VMI today. His analysis of military topics—including the stress he gave to such necessities as discipline and mobility in the field, and the importance of efficient artillery when used along with flexible infantry maneuvers—were vital for the soldier of his time and those of today.

Although Jackson's lessons may have been timely and on point, his delivery was not. He had a grasp of the subject matter, but he was a poor instructor when it came to his delivery in the classroom. He memorized his lectures and then recited them to his students. His field of study was difficult, even to the nineteenth-century student. If a cadet came to him out of class to ask questions, Jackson merely recited his lecture again. Should a student press him further, he would lose his cool, threatening the student with punishment for disobedience. Francis H. Smith, who served as VMI's superintendent while Jackson taught, summarized his professor's performance in his book *History of the Virginia Military Institute*:

> As Professor of Natural and Experimental Philosophy, Major Jackson was not a success. He had not the qualifications needed for so important a chair. He was no teacher, and he lacked the tact required in getting along with his classes. . . . His genius was in the Science and Art of War. He found a field for the display of this genius when the war opened in 1861.

Add Jackson's odd character to the mix, and students often had a difficult time taking their professor seriously. His poor performances in the classroom made him the target of constant pranks by students. Members of the VMI alumni appealed to the academy's board of visitors in 1856, requesting the removal of Jackson from his position. The attempt failed, but their efforts put a brighter spotlight on an academic career that was floundering.

Still, all was not a failure for Jackson while he lived in Lexington and taught at VMI. In 1853, he courted and married Elinor Junkin, whom he lovingly referred to as "Ellie." She was the daughter of George Junkin, the president of another school in Lexington, Washington College. That college would later be known as Washington and Lee University, after Robert E. Lee, who served as the school's president following the

Civil War. President Junkin even expanded his college residence to provide a place for the Jacksons to live. When Robert E. Lee presided over the college during the late 1860s, he lived in that same house, which is today known as the Lee-Jackson House.

The Jacksons' marriage did not last long, for Ellie died the following year in October during the birth of a stillborn child. The double loss was catastrophic for Jackson, who left the country the following summer and went abroad, traveling through Belgium, France, Germany, Switzerland, England, and Scotland. After his return, Jackson was soon courting another woman, Mary Anna Morrison from North Carolina, the daughter of yet another college president. Robert Hall Morrison was the retired head of Davidson College.

The couple married on July 16, 1857, but tragedy found Jackson yet again. Mary Anna delivered a child on April 30, 1858, but the baby died less than a month later. There would be another child, a daughter. Julia Laura Jackson was born in November 1862, while her father was fighting under the command of Robert E. Lee. Jackson would not live to see his child reach her first birthday, as he was killed just six months later.

JACKSON AND RACE

Although Jackson may have performed poorly in the classrooms at VMI, he was the center of another educational effort. While attending his local Presbyterian church, he was responsible for establishing Sunday school classes for local black children. He and Mary Anna worked at this ministry together. As Mary Anna later recalled in her memoirs, Thomas "preferred that my labors should be given to the colored children, believing that it was more important and useful to put the strong hand of the Gospel under the ignorant African race, to lift them up." While Jackson may not have believed that blacks were equal to whites, he treated them well and wanted them to succeed.

Historian James Robertson noted the later writings of a local Presbyterian minister, Dr. William Spottswood White: "In their religious instruction he succeeded wonderfully. His discipline was systematic and firm, but very kind. . . . His servants reverenced and loved him, as they would have done a brother or father. . . . He was emphatically the black man's friend." In an age when many whites would not support teaching blacks or providing them with the means of self-improvement, Thomas Jackson dedicated himself to those goals. He called his Sunday school students by their given names, and they would refer to their Bible school teacher as "Marse [Mister] Major."

In the world of the nineteenth-century South, race relations, due to the institution of slavery, were complicated and favored whites. Jackson may have been a "black man's friend," but he was also a slave owner. During the late 1850s, the Jackson family owned six slaves. The Jacksons received three of them as a wedding present, including a mother, Hetty, and her two teen-aged sons, Cyrus and George. Jackson had purchased the fourth, Albert, at the slave's request. Albert made a deal with his new owner to work off the purchase price and gain his freedom. Jackson did not work Albert, but instead "loaned" him out as a waiter at a Lexington hotel, as well as to VMI. A fifth slave, a woman named Amy, also asked Jackson to purchase her at a local slave auction so she could serve as the family cook and housekeeper. The last, a four-year-old orphan girl named Emma, had a learning disability and was bought by Jackson as a gift to his wife.

What, exactly, was Thomas Jackson's view of slavery? The answer is not clear. Historian James Robertson, in his biography of Stonewall Jackson, tried to summarize Jackson's relationship with slavery:

> Jackson neither apologized for nor spoke in favor of the practice of slavery. He probably opposed the institution. Yet in his mind the Creator had sanctioned slavery, and

man had no moral right to challenge its existence. The good Christian slaveholder was one who treated his servants fairly and humanely at all times.

It is known that, during the Civil War, Thomas Jackson either sold off his slaves or hired them out to work for others. This is addressed by Mary Anna in her memoirs, when she states that "our servants . . . without the firm guidance and restraint of their master, the excitement of the times proved so demoralizing to them that he deemed it best for me to provide them with good homes among the permanent residents."

THE APPROACH OF WAR

By 1859, the Jacksons took residence at the only house Thomas ever owned during his years in Lexington. It was a brick townhouse located at 8 East Washington Street. He and Mary Anna lived there for two years until he went off to fight during the Civil War. He would never live in that house again.

Later in 1859, Virginia witnessed the attempted slave rebellion led by fiery abolitionist John Brown. Robert E. Lee would play a crucial role in ending that rebellion and apprehending Brown. During his trial, Brown was found guilty and sentenced to hang. Thomas Jackson attended the hanging. The Virginia governor had requested the presence of cadets at the execution, and VMI's Major William Gilham delivered a group from the academy to Charles Town, Virginia, as an additional military unit at Brown's execution, which took place December 2. That day, Major Jackson led a unit of artillery, including a pair of howitzers, along with 21 cadets. Among the VMI cadets at Brown's hanging was John Wilkes Booth, who, less than six years later, would assassinate President Abraham Lincoln.

A year later, the ongoing struggle between the North and South over the expansion of slavery finally came to a head with the election of Republican Abraham Lincoln, from Illinois.

During his teaching career at the Virginia Military Institute, Stonewall Jackson led a group of cadets from the school to Charles Town, Virginia, to witness the execution of John Brown (above) for his role in the raid on Harpers Ferry. Jackson, who was not outspoken about his views on slavery, sympathized with Brown and had even petitioned for the abolitionist to be spared from death.

Soon, Southern states began seceding from the Union, including Virginia, following the Confederate attack against the federal installation at Charleston Harbor, Fort Sumter.

Within days of Virginia's secession and its joining with the Confederacy, Jackson was summoned to Richmond. The VMI Corps of Cadets had been ordered to the Virginia capital to become drillmasters to the thousands of young men who were

"Let Us Cross Over the River"

General Robert E. Lee gained a great victory in the Battle of Chancellorsville, fought in late April and early May of 1863. But the field of battle had been won at a great cost, with 12,700 men counted as casualties. The most crucial among them, the one whom Robert E. Lee could not afford to lose, was General Thomas "Stonewall" Jackson.

Jackson had been wounded on the evening of May 2, following his successful advance through the Wilderness and the early evening attack on Hooker's right flank. In the darkness, around 9 P.M., Hooker and a group of staff officers and messengers had ridden along the Orange Plank Road just a mile from Hooker's headquarters at Chancellorsville. When cannon fire struck the road, Jackson and his men rode into the thick forest. This move placed the Confederate officers near Rebel picket lines.

Out of the darkness, picket fire struck the Confederate officers on their horses. One of Jackson's men shouted to the confused soldiers, "Cease firing! You are firing into your own men!" Disbelieving the order, the pickets fired again, this time hitting Jackson three times—once in the right hand and twice in the left arm. Jackson's frightened horse turned toward Union lines, galloping toward the enemy. Several low tree branches nearly knocked the wounded Rebel general off his horse before a staff member stopped the blind gallop.

The wounds were severe. Hours later, field surgeons removed Jackson's arm. Two days later, the general was removed from the field and sent to recover at Guiney's Station, Virginia. He seemed to be recovering well through the following days. But, on May 7, he was diagnosed with pneumonia. Three days later, the fiercely religious Confederate died. His final words were as emotional as they were curious, words recalled in Peter Earle's biography of Lee: "Let us cross over the river and rest under the shade of the trees."

enlisting in the Rebel military. Jackson, having been advanced in rank to colonel, was placed in command of these cadets. A week later, on April 27, Virginia governor John Letcher handed orders to Colonel Jackson to take a military unit west to capture the federal arsenal at Harpers Ferry, which had been abolitionist John Brown's goal just 18 months earlier.

Once in control of the former Union facility, Jackson began forming the military command that would come to be known as the Stonewall Brigade, which included the 2nd, 4th, 5th, 27th, and 33rd Virginia Infantry regiments. Recruits were assembled largely from Virginia's Shenandoah Valley region. During his years at VMI, Jackson had talked of military matters, the importance of discipline, and tactics on the battlefield. Now he was using those same skills and martial values in real life in his own brigade. He became well known and was even hated by some of his men for his constant military drilling. Few units became more disciplined in a fight than those who marched under Thomas Jackson. By June 17, 1861, Jackson had been promoted to brigadier general.

The following month, Jackson earned the nickname that is remembered today. When Union and Rebel forces engaged in battle at Bull Run, near Manassas, Virginia, on a hot July day, Northern forces almost succeeded in taking the field and defeating the Southern army. In the midst of the fight, General Jackson ordered his men to hold their positions. Another Confederate general noted to his men, as recalled by historian Geoffrey Ward, how Jackson was "standing like a stonewall." These words of praise offered in the heat of battle would be remembered, and Jackson would become a legend.

JACKSON'S "FOOT CAVALRY"

Throughout 1862, Jackson continued to make a name for himself as a Confederate military leader. He was not always successful on the field of battle, however. During the weeklong engagement known as the Seven Days, fought in late June and early July, he did not command his men well, managing to get them into position late on the battlefield more than once. But, earlier that spring, he had performed brilliantly more than once against the enemy.

Jackson was one of the South's most unique generals. He was both odd and extremely religious. He often ate foods he could not stand, thinking them to be the key to health. During battles, he was remembered for sucking lemons. His religious beliefs were passionate. A devout observer of the Sabbath, Jackson refused to send or even read a letter on Sunday. He had what was called a Joshua complex, believing his army to be an extension of God's wrath. In his words, as noted by historian Geoffrey Ward, his was "an army of the living God, as well as of its country."

As a commander, Jackson's men did not like him much. He was a stern military leader, a harsh general who forced his men to march daily anywhere from 25 to 40 miles (40 to 65 km). Some referred to Jackson's infantry as "foot cavalry." One infantryman summed up his commander by saying, according to historian Ward: "All old Jackson gave us was a musket, a hundred rounds, and a gum blanket and he druv (sic) us like Hell." But he was a brilliant tactician on the battlefield. During the early summer of 1862, as Union commander George B. McClellan moved 200,000 men onto the James River peninsula east of Richmond to mount a massive campaign, General Lee sent Jackson and 20,000 Confederates into the Shenandoah Valley to keep several other Union armies busy.

The Shenandoah Valley was rich farm country, the breadbasket of the South. The valley is located in Virginia, west of the Blue Ridge, the easternmost spine of the Appalachian Mountains. From the valley, Jackson could move about easily, using the Blue Ridge to hide his actions, then emerge into the eastern portion of Virginia to meet his next enemy. Three Union armies were kept off balance by Jackson's brilliant movements. These

Union armies represented a combined force of 75,000 men. As Jackson weaved and dodged his way up and down the valley, these armies were never able to control his movements and defeat him in the field. Union forces chased Jackson through farming towns from Winchester to Front Royal to Cross Keys to Port Republic. But Jackson, using a huge map that measured more than 8 feet (2.4 m) in length, would engage them, often sending Union forces into retreat and melting away to fight another day.

Only once, during a spring engagement at Kernstown, did Jackson lose a battle during the campaign in the valley. Jackson was philosophical as well as practical about his field tactics. Historian Ward noted Jackson's words: "Always mystify, mislead, and surprise the enemy if possible; and when you strike and overcome him, never let up in the pursuit so long as your men have the strength to follow." Later in the war, it would be a Union commander, Ulysses S. Grant, who would appear to follow Jackson's approach to the battlefield when he met General Lee in a series of battles in Virginia in 1864.

Late in the summer of 1862, Jackson furthered his legacy as one of the South's greatest Civil War generals during the fighting at Second Bull Run. On August 29 and 30, Lee's and Jackson's armies fought Union commander John Pope and his Army of the Potomac. During the first day of fighting, Jackson made his army appear weak, encouraging an attack from Pope. The desired Union assault followed, and Pope's men hit the Rebel line hard, but failed to break it. At one point, when some Confederate soldiers ran low on ammunition, they tossed rocks at the enemy. Encouraged by the day's action, Pope sent a telegraph to President Lincoln assuring him the Confederates were on the run.

On the morning of August 30, Pope attacked Jackson once more, but Lee sent his men forward—30,000 troops under the command of General James Longstreet—and the Rebels pushed Pope back. The scope of the battle was immense, as Longstreet's

Stonewall Jackson's military performance in the Civil War elevated his status from man to myth. He led his famed and feared Stonewall Brigade into major conflicts and often emerged victorious, most notably so in the Shenandoah Valley campaign. In the Battle of Chancellorsville, Jackson was injured and lost his left arm, causing Lee to remark, "He has lost his left arm, but I have lost my right." Above, the last meeting between General Robert E. Lee (right) and Stonewall Jackson (left).

five divisions hit the Union men along a front 2 miles (3 km) long. As the Union broke from the fight, Southern forces delivered a shower of artillery that fully insulted the retreating enemy.

Looking at the tally sheet for the summer of 1862, the South had made great achievements on the battlefield. By the final days of August, western Virginia was out from under Union control, McClellan's campaign had been lost, Pope had been disgraced by his mismanagement of Second Bull Run, and Jackson had marched rings around his Union opponents. The only Northern troops within a hundred miles of Richmond, as one observer noted, were prisoners.

Jackson had proven himself an invaluable officer to General Lee. He would further that reputation the next September during the Battle of Antietam, when his hurried arrival to the battlefield from Harpers Ferry helped save Lee's army from annihilation. He would again prove himself during the fight at Fredericksburg in December.

But Jackson's legacy was cut short the following spring. With Lee's army of 60,000 facing a Union force of 135,000 men, Jackson helped turn the tide of the fight at Chancellorsville in early May. He proposed a march through 15 miles (24 km) of dense undergrowth along a narrow trail unknown to Union troops. Although the move split Lee's forces, Jackson successfully delivered 25,000 men around Union commander Joseph Hooker's forces, smashing into the Federal leader's right flank by complete surprise. From that point in the battle, Hooker remained off balance, ultimately losing.

The victory, however, came at a terrible loss. Later on the day of the march, Jackson was accidentally shot by Confederate soldiers, a victim of friendly fire. Jackson would never recover from his wounds and died several days later, ending his brilliant days of mystifying, misleading, and surprising the enemy.

Frederick Douglass

His mother, Harriet, had picked out his name long before he was born: Frederick Augustus Washington Baily (or Bailey). Only later in his life would he be known as Frederick Douglass. The exact date of his birth is not certain, only that he was born in February of 1818 in Maryland, just a few miles from the eastern shores of Chesapeake Bay. Frederick came into the world as the son of a slave woman and a white father, whose identity is not clear. Perhaps it was his mother's owner, Aaron Anthony. As an adult, Douglass stated repeatedly that he knew almost nothing about his father.

Since his mother was a field hand in the cornfields of Anthony's Holmes Hill Farm, she did not see her new child much. He was sent to live with his grandmother, Betsey Baily, who lived a few miles from Holmes Hill, where she had already raised Harriet's earlier children. During his early years growing up in his grandmother's cabin, young Frederick did not know he was a slave.

Then, at age six, his grandmother took him on a long walk. During their journey, according to historian Sandra Thomas, Frederick clung "to his grandmother's skirt with fear and uncertainty." While his first six years had been spent in his grandmother's care, the next six would be marked by separation and loss. He was taken to the Lloyd Plantation. Edward Lloyd V was one of the wealthiest men in Maryland, and he employed Aaron Anthony as a manager at his estate. Frederick learned he was to work as a slave there. As his grandmother left him, young Frederick dropped to the ground in sorrow and wept.

Life at his new home was filled with misery and fear. One dark night, Frederick woke up to the sounds of a woman screaming. He found a crack in the wall of the kitchen, where he slept, and saw Aaron Anthony whipping his aunt, Hester Baily. Although the beating frightened the young boy, he forced himself to watch. He would witness other slave beatings during the years that followed.

By age seven, Frederick's mother, Harriet, died. Since he rarely saw her, he was not informed of her death until years later. Frederick was not entirely alone as a slave working at the Lloyd Plantation. He was such a likeable boy that he was selected to play with the youngest Lloyd boy, Daniel. There were times, however, when Frederick had to go work in the farm fields, as well.

Frederick was also a favorite of Lucretia Auld, the daughter of Aaron Anthony. In 1826, at the age of eight, Frederick was sent to live in Baltimore to work for Lucretia's brother-in-law, Hugh Auld, who ran a shipbuilding company there. Before leaving for Baltimore, Lucretia told Frederick that, if he washed himself up clean, she would give him his first pair of pants.

AN OPPORTUNITY FOR LITERACY

Life in Baltimore was quite different for Frederick than it had been on the Maryland farm. He was in a large city, one of the largest in the South. His work was simple, mostly consisting of running errands for the Auld family and seeing to the family's baby, little Tommy. The house's mistress, Sophia Auld, was a highly religious woman and insisted that Frederick be treated kindly.

Often, Frederick would notice Sophia reading aloud from a Bible, which interested him greatly. Boldly, he one day asked her to teach him to read. Although such a thing was not only frowned upon by white Southerners but was also illegal, she agreed. A quick learner, Frederick soon mastered his ABCs and picked up several words. When Sophia's husband, Hugh, learned of her teaching the young slave to read, he was angry. Slaves who learn to read became difficult, he said; they would not continue to work, but would feel as though there was more to life than just being a slave. Hugh Auld instructed Sophia to stop her lessons at once with young Frederick.

But a seed had been planted, and Frederick had no intention of letting it die if he could help it. He continued to work at his reading on the sly, learning more words from poor white children he met locally and during his errand runs. Hugh's response had told the insightful Frederick that reading and literacy were the keys to a better future. Although Sophia had at first not seen the harm in teaching her young slave to read, she became upset when she caught him reading any books or papers.

Slowly, willfully, Frederick Douglass learned to read. By age 12, having earned a small amount of money through running family errands, he secretly bought a copy of a collection of patriotic speeches and other writings on democracy, freedom, and human rights. Through his ever-increasing literacy, Frederick was learning more than his master and mistress could ever imagine. Through his reading, along with the material he read about liberty, young Frederick Douglass learned to despise slavery.

NEW CHANGES

Before he turned 13, Frederick's young life took another turn. Aaron Anthony died, and his property, including Frederick and other slaves, was passed on to his children, including Lucretia Auld. Soon, Frederick was sent back to the Lloyd Plantation. When the property was divided among Lucretia and her two brothers, she chose to keep Frederick, and she then sent him back to Hugh and Sophia Auld. During the settling of the estate, Frederick was not only separated again from other family members, but he also witnessed his aged grandmother being thrown out of her cabin and abandoned. She would soon die alone in a local forest. This only hardened Frederick's hatred of slavery.

Death continued to alter Frederick's circumstances. A year later, Lucretia Auld died and her husband, Thomas, gained ownership of Frederick, now 15 years old. Thomas treated his slaves poorly, barely feeding them. His slaves, including Frederick, were forced to take food from slaves living at nearby farms and plantations. During this time, the teenaged Frederick was hired out to a white farmer named Freeman. While at the Freeman farm, Douglass, who had become reasonably skilled in his reading and writing, taught other area slaves to read the New Testament at a Sunday school held at the farm. As for Freeman, who knew of the reading classes, he did not seem concerned. Other local white slave owners were concerned, though. During one Sunday school class, a group of whites armed with clubs entered and broke up the reading session.

By now, Frederick was extremely unhappy with his circumstances. He was working as a field hand and being beaten for his disobedience on a regular basis. Thomas Auld was having so much trouble with his young slave that, just before Frederick turned 16, Auld sent him to work for Edward Covey, a poor white farmer who had a local reputation as a "slave breaker." While Frederick had hated his treatment at the hands of Thomas Auld, he despised Covey, even though he did eat better than under Auld's ownership. The fieldwork was endless, and Covey whipped his slaves regularly. He would even hide behind bushes and watch to see which of his slaves were not working

Frederick Douglass was born a slave on Maryland's eastern shore. Named Frederick Baily, the young boy taught himself how to read while working in several households before running away to Massachusetts. Determined to continue his self-education, Douglass discovered The Liberator, *an abolitionist newspaper that inspired him to become a civil rights activist.*

hard enough, and then mark them for a beating. Frederick received his first beating within his first week at the Covey farm.

As the months went by, the teenaged Frederick was beaten so often that, as he would later write in his memoirs, he was almost psychologically broken. Then, on a hot August afternoon, after Frederick collapsed in the field from overwork, Covey attacked him, kicking the boy as he lay on the ground. Angered and frustrated, Frederick later went back to Thomas Auld, asking him to take him back. Thomas refused. When Frederick returned to the Covey farm, his owner began tying him up for beatings.

From somewhere deep inside himself, young Frederick could take no more. As he would later note in his memoirs: "I seized Covey hard by the throat, and as I did so, I rose." Overseer and slave engaged in a fight that lasted for two hours until Covey gave in. Humiliated, Covey told Frederick that his beating would have been less painful if he had cooperated. The fact was, Douglass remembered years later, "that he had not whipped me at all." After that encounter, Covey never tried to whip Frederick Douglass again. Frederick had learned an important lesson that day, as he would later write: "Men are whipped oftenest who are whipped easiest."

THE SIREN CALL OF FREEDOM

Frederick continued to be "farmed out" to Covey for a year or so. Then he was sent to another planter, William Freeland. Freeland was a breath of fresh air for Frederick, since he treated his slaves kindly. Douglass found himself in circumstances that allowed him to establish another school for teaching fellow slaves to read. The group met on Sundays, when they did not work, and also during secret meetings under cover of darkness.

Frederick Douglass, who was nearly 18 years old, was no longer interested in being a slave under any circumstances. He and a handful of other slaves began planning their escapes.

After working for Freeland for a year, Douglass and his fellow conspirators launched their plan, which called for them to steal a boat, row north up the bay, and reach freedom in Pennsylvania. They set Easter 1836 as the date. But before they could put their plans in motion, one of Douglass's fellow plotters told their plans to some white men. The men caught the slaves and placed them in a local jail, where Frederick remained for a week. He anticipated his days in Maryland were over and that his punishment would be to be sold into the Deep South. But he was wrong. Thomas Auld took him home and then sent him to his brother Hugh in Baltimore to work. Assuming Frederick would try and escape again, Thomas promised Frederick he would free him at age 25, if he worked hard.

But Frederick returned to Baltimore a different man. For one, he was 18 years old, no longer a boy in any way. He stood 6 feet (1.8 m) tall and would never see a farm field again. Hugh decided to apprentice him out for training as a ship caulker. After a year, Frederick was earning as much for his labor as any other tradesman working at his level. In Baltimore, he came into contact with free blacks, some of whom were educated. He joined a black educational forum called the East Baltimore Mental Improvement Society. It was with this group that Frederick sharpened his skills of logic and rhetoric. He engaged in lively debates with his fellow society members. It was also through the society, and at church, that he met a free black woman named Anna Murray. Although she was not well educated, she was religious and industrious. The two fell in love and became engaged in 1838.

But all was not right in the life of Frederick Douglass. He might have been in love, enjoying intellectual banter with the society, earning wages, and working as a skilled tradesman. But he was still a slave. Although Thomas Auld had promised him his freedom, Frederick did not intend to take his chances by biding his time until age 25. He resolved, once again, to try and escape to freedom. He set a date of September 3, 1838, after a serious argument with Hugh Auld.

His plan was basically straightforward, requiring no secret journey by boat at night. He borrowed money from Anna and purchased a train ticket to Philadelphia. Needing the papers of a free black man, he borrowed a "sailor's protection" from a friend, a set of documents that identified the bearer as a free black seaman. He even made certain he would not be questioned by wearing a red sailor's shirt and black cravat. On the train, he waited anxiously for the conductor to check his papers. His appearance did not fully match that of the owner of the documents. But when he offered them to the railroad employee, they were given only a quick glance. Frederick Douglass was on the way to freedom. When the train arrived in Wilmington, Delaware (a slave state), he took a ferry across the river to Philadelphia where he immediately took another train, this one bound for New York City.

By September 4, he arrived in his disguise, a free man. His whole anxious adventure had taken less than 24 hours. As he would later write in his memoirs, "A new world had opened upon me . . . Anguish and grief, like darkness and rain, may be depicted, but gladness and joy, like the rainbow, defy the skill of pen or pencil." Anna soon joined Frederick in New York and the two married on September 15.

BECOMING AN ABOLITIONIST

Frederick and Anna did not settle down in New York, but moved instead to Massachusetts, where they took residence at New Bedford. He could get work in the seaport as a ship caulker. It was here that Frederick changed his name, since slave catchers would be looking for him. At the time, he and Anna were staying with Nathan Johnson, a prosperous black resident of New Bedford. As Johnson was reading Walter Scott's novel *The*

Lady of the Lake, he suggested that Frederick take the name of one of the novel's characters. Frederick Baily became Frederick Douglass.

Free and happily married, Douglass found life both exciting and difficult in New Bedford. Schools were integrated and churches hosted whites and blacks. But some places were closed to blacks, and white employers did not always hire blacks. In fact, Douglass could not find work as a caulker, as white shipyard workers did not like to work next to black workers. Freedom may have been his new lot, but Douglass had to work unskilled jobs including digging root cellars, cutting firewood, and other day labor work. Anna took in laundry for money. By the summer of 1839, Anna and Frederick had their first child, a girl they named Rosetta. The next year brought a son named Lewis. The family made a place for themselves in New Bedford, despite the disappointments. Douglass became extremely involved in the local black community, serving as a minister at the black Zion Methodist Church.

It was in New Bedford that Frederick Douglass was introduced first-hand to the world of abolitionism. Abolitionists were those who opposed the existence of slavery and sought to have the institution immediately ended, or abolished. Just months after arriving in the Massachusetts seaport, he discovered the abolitionist newspaper *The Liberator*, which was published and edited by one of the North's most famous antislavery advocates, William Lloyd Garrison. The abolitionist publication inspired Douglass, who later wrote in his memoirs: "The paper became my meat and drink . . . My soul was set all on fire."

Douglass not only subscribed to *The Liberator*, he also began attending abolitionist meetings. In 1839, he spoke against the African colonization effort, which was then promoted by white Southerners who were suggesting that free blacks be sent back to Africa, rather than be allowed to live free in the United States. Some of his arguments against the movement found their way to the pages of Garrison's antislavery newspaper.

TELLING HIS STORY

In 1841, Douglass attended a meeting of the Bristol Anti-Slavery Society and heard Garrison speak in person. The two men met that same evening. Douglass later wrote in his autobiography how "no face and form ever impressed me with such sentiments [of the hatred of slavery] as did those of William Lloyd Garrison." Garrison was impressed with Douglass, as well, and wrote about him in a later issue of *The Liberator*. Douglass was so inspired that he soon gave his own antislavery speech to the Massachusetts Anti-Slavery Society's annual convention held in Nantucket, Massachusetts. The experience was new to Douglass. He later remembered how his legs shook nervously as he spoke in front of the audience. In his speech, he recounted some of his experiences as a slave.

Those who heard Frederick Douglass speak often gave special notice to not only his words and message, but to his appearance and poise. "As a speaker, he has few equals," wrote one Concord, Massachusetts, newspaper, as noted by historian Sandra Thomas. "He has wit, arguments, sarcasm, pathos—all that first rate men show in their master effort." Some witnesses to a Douglass lecture noted his bright, flashing eyes; his broad mass of dark, springy hair; and his height. He was an impressive man to watch and hear.

Other speaking engagements followed his first lecture. Two years later, Douglass was a speaker for the American Anti-Slavery Society's Hundred Conventions Project, a six-month-long tour that held engagements at meeting and convention halls throughout the East and Midwest. Slowly, but deliberately, Frederick Douglass was making a name for himself on the lecture circuit as an inspiring orator.

His message rang clear. Douglass went to great lengths to paint vivid, hard pictures for his audiences, who listened spellbound. He talked of brutal beatings, not only against his person, but also upon children and older women. He railed in a strong

"The last time Fred saw his mother."   "Colonel Lloyd whipping old Barney."   "The overseer, Gore, shooting Denby."

Encouraged by abolitionists like William Lloyd Garrison, Frederick Douglass began speaking in public about his experiences as a slave. He spoke in detail regarding practices of slave owners and overseers while also recounting his own brutal experiences in bondage. Hoping to further publicize the evils of slavery, Douglass penned his autobiography, Narrative of the Life of Frederick Douglass, an American Slave, Written By Himself. *Above, illustrations from Frederick Douglass's autobiography depict the emotional and physical damage exacted by slavery.*

voice against harsh living conditions for the South's slaves and of young slave children who were malnourished and covered with sores. He nearly scandalized white genteel society with tales of how slave owners "bred" with their female slaves. Douglass even brought on laughter when he told how he had finally stood up to Edward Covey and brought an end to his beatings.

In 1845, the increasingly famous Douglass took the next step in telling his personal story of slavery and eventual freedom. In 1845, his autobiography was published. Titled *Narrative of the Life of Frederick Douglass, an American Slave*, Douglass, then just 27 years old, found an interested audience. It became an immediate success, selling 11,000 copies during its first three years in print, which included nine printings. Not only did his life story sell in the North, but it sold in Europe, too, where it was translated into French and Dutch. Some critics and doubters found Douglass's book so eloquently written they could not believe a former slave had penned it.

But the publication of Douglass's story proved a potential threat to him, as well. Some of his friends thought his former owners might recognize him through his writings. As a precaution, he was encouraged to travel abroad for a while. Over the next two years, beginning in August 1845, Douglass lived in Great Britain and Ireland. He continued to speak in opposition to slavery, only in front of British and Irish crowds. He found new supporters among the English, including the aged abolitionist Thomas Clarkson, one of the few remaining survivors to have fought to end British-supported slavery. Another supporter, Ellen Richardson of Newcastle, helped raise £700 to help buy Douglass's official freedom from Hugh Auld. Once the agreement was secured, the papers were handed over to a delighted Frederick Douglass.

BACK TO THE STATES

Now internationally famous as one of the most eloquent black speakers against slavery, and officially free, Frederick Douglass returned to the United States and took up work editing for a series of abolitionist newspapers, including *The North Star* and *Frederick Douglass Weekly*. Douglass included a motto for *The North Star*: "Right is of no Sex—Truth is of no Color—God is the Father of us all, and we are all brethren." While Douglass poured much of his professional efforts into pushing for abolition, he also advocated other causes that were important to him. These included equal rights for women, including the right to vote, and desegregation of schools. He also fought hard for more even distribution of school funding. In New York City, for example, there were 2 or 3 black students for every 100 white students, a ratio of 1 to 40. Yet the city's funding ratio for blacks to whites was about 1 to 1,500! The money put into black education was far inferior to that invested in white schools.

During the fall of 1847, Douglass went on yet another speaking tour. By the time he returned to New Bedford, he had made the decision to move his family to Rochester, New York. There he would publish a new abolitionist newspaper, one that would no longer have to directly compete with other antislavery presses in New England. In fact, tension had developed between Douglass and William Lloyd Garrison. The sticking point was a shift in Douglass's thinking concerning abolition. Garrison had always been an advocate of nonviolence. His campaign had been fought with a pen, not a sword. But Douglass began to consider the merits of violence carried out in the name of such an ideal as abolition.

Earlier in the year, Douglass had met one of the most outspoken advocates of antislavery violence in the country—the fiery John Brown. Brown did not believe that writing or speaking against slavery would ultimately bring down the hated institution. It would take more—acts intended to stir strong emotions against slavery, including violence against those who supported it. As historian Sandra Thomas noted, Brown believed that those who owned slaves "had forfeited their right to live, and that slaves had the right to gain their liberty in any way they could." Douglass began including in his writings his personal support of violence against slavery, even admitting he relished hearing of slave rebellions against Southerners. This shift in strategy did not sit well with Garrison and other abolitionists.

Garrison and Douglass had a final split in the summer of 1851 at the annual meeting of the American Anti-Slavery Society, which Garrison had helped create nearly 20 years earlier. Douglass spoke out in favor of his abolitionist followers turning to politics as a tool against slavery. Abolitionists should run for office, vote for antislavery candidates, and encourage politicians to pass laws that restricted slavery, he said. Garrison and his advocates were outraged, as he had always spoken against the political system as a tool of the pro-slavery advocates. Almost immediately, Garrison's supporters launched a campaign against Douglass, but the black leader did not focus on such criticisms.

During the 1850s, as the United States further split over the issue of slavery, Douglass continued to hammer away against slavery. Early in the decade, he became directly involved in the Underground Railroad, a secret system of safe houses where escaped slaves could hide out by day and move toward freedom by night. The system extended from the upper South all the way to Canada. From his home in Rochester, Douglass was close to the New York border with Canada. His house became one of the last stops on the Underground Railroad before an escaped slave reached ultimate freedom across the Canadian border. After awhile, Douglass became the superintendent of the Underground Railroad system in his region. There were times when nearly a dozen escaped black men and women might be hiding in the Douglass house. Throughout the 1850s, Douglass helped hundreds of slaves on their way to the North.

REFUSING SUPPORT

By the mid-1850s, the slavery issue was the hottest political topic in the United States. Congress debated where slavery might expand to west of the Mississippi River, and the number of people opposed to slavery grew each year. John Brown became embroiled in more violence out in Kansas when the future of the territory—whether it would ultimately become a slave state or a free state—seemed uncertain. Brown and his small band of followers killed several pro-slavery men in 1856.

By 1859, Brown was in Virginia, plotting another violent strategy. He had worked up an unlikely scheme involving a raid on the federal arsenal at Harpers Ferry, where he and his supporters intended to capture a large supply of guns. They could then use these weapons to arm slaves in the region and bring about a massive slave uprising. Wanting Douglass's support for his plan, he requested a meeting with the black leader in Chambersburg, Pennsylvania, in August. Douglass went and heard all about Brown's plan. Fearing it would fail and only succeed in antagonizing the South further, Douglass refused to support or join Brown.

Two months later, on October 16, Brown carried out his plan. Although he and his men managed to capture the arsenal, they were soon surrounded by townspeople, followed by the state militia, then U.S. Marines. The raid ended the following day, with several of Brown's collaborators being killed, including two of his sons, and he was arrested. As news of the Brown raid on Harpers Ferry began to spread across the country, Douglass was in Philadelphia lecturing. Friends contacted Douglass to inform him that letters had been discovered suggesting the black leader had been involved in the raid and attempted slave rebellion. One of Brown's captured followers stated that Douglass had indeed been part of the plan and that the black abolitionist had promised to send reinforcements to aid Brown at Harpers Ferry. Soon, northern newspapers ran stories accusing Douglass.

This was a situation that Douglass could not ignore. He feared he might be arrested. Even though he had not participated in the raid, he had known about it beforehand and had not tried to stop it or inform authorities. Douglass was so concerned that he left the country for Canada. There he wrote letters of his own, explaining why he had gone abroad and how he had refused to cooperate with Brown's scheme. He stated that he could not have advocated an attack against federal property, despite his general advocacy of violent means to end slavery. Yet, even as he condemned the raid itself, according to historian Sandra Thomas, Douglass wrote high praise for Brown, calling him "a noble old hero." A month following the Brown raid,

Douglass set sail for England for a speaking tour that he had scheduled long before the raid. There, with stories of Brown's raid circulating, Douglass was a hero to many who came to hear him speak.

While Douglass rode the wave of enthusiastic support in England, he made plans to travel to France and speak the following spring. But tragedy struck in May when he received word from Rochester that his youngest daughter, Annie, had died. With this painful news, Douglass cancelled his tour and set out for home. He reentered the country through Canada, to avoid detection by authorities.

THE COMING OF WAR

By 1860, despite Frederick Douglass's nonstop campaign to bring down slavery in the United States, abolitionism had made only slight dents in the institution. But change was in the wind that year for the movement that was so dear to the former slave. Political events finally came to a head as the new Republican Party, created as a political force opposed to the expansion of slavery into the western territories, managed to elect Abraham Lincoln from Illinois to the presidency. Although Lincoln was no abolitionist, slavery-supporting Southerners saw him as a radical who would fight to limit slavery. Driven by strong political emotions, Southern states began seceding from the Union by December.

In the spring of 1861, war finally broke out between the South and the North. In April, an attack by Confederates against a federal fort in Charleston Harbor, South Carolina, opened the deadly conflict that would continue over the next four years. As the country split, abolitionists such as Douglass and Garrison were partially blamed for creating a hostile climate by speaking out against slavery and the South. With the war on, newly in-augurated President Lincoln rallied the North militarily in an effort to restore the divided country. Southerners, meanwhile, fought to establish their own nation where slavery would not only fail to be criticized, but would be protected.

As for Frederick Douglass, he had his own goals for the war. He established two specifically: 1) to make the war, in part, about ending slavery, and 2) to support the rights of black men to join the Union Army and fight. Lincoln did not, during the opening months of the war, support the goal of ending slavery, but he, as well as many others across the North, eventually came around to Douglass's initial goals. Just as Douglass had traveled the lecture circuit before the war in opposition to slavery, he continued to speak out, encouraging President Lincoln to add emancipation to his war aims.

During the first year of the war, Lincoln was reluctant to make any clear moves against slavery. One of his chief concerns was that four slave states—Missouri, Kentucky, Maryland, and Delaware—had not seceded along with their fellow slave states. They had not joined the Confederacy, but had remained within the Union. Lincoln fretted that, should the border states leave the Union, it would make prosecuting the war that much more difficult, regardless of what goals he might or might not support.

By April 16, 1862, with the war a year old, the president signed his first bill into law that was intended to strike a blow against slavery. This new law banned slavery in Washington, D.C. His public efforts, for the moment, stopped there. When several Union commanders took steps to confiscate slaves in regions of the Confederacy that had come under federal control, Lincoln overturned those military orders. Even a year into the war, the president was still concerned about the border states.

Yet abolitionists, among them Frederick Douglass, continued to campaign in favor of making the war about ending slavery. Douglass spoke equally loudly in favor of arming Northern blacks for military service. Lincoln seemed unmoved. But the spring and summer of 1862 brought significant defeats on the battlefield for the Union. These included a poorly coordinated campaign along Virginia's James River Peninsula intended to capture the Confederate capital at Richmond, as well as a second battle at Bull Run, Virginia. The war was proving increasingly costly in manpower, and when a draft began, Northern cities experienced draft riots.

The Confederates fought tooth and nail, leading Lincoln to decide he would have to take even more significant and drastic measures against the South to damage its resolve and ability to wage war. By late summer of 1862, he was prepared to issue an executive order that would free all slaves in regions of the South not under federal control. But when he read his intended Emancipation Proclamation to his cabinet members, they insisted he wait to make it public after Union armies achieved a significant victory on the battlefield. Otherwise, they argued, the proclamation would ring hollow.

Fortunately, Lincoln, his cabinet, and abolitionists such as Frederick Douglass did not have to wait long. On September 17, an immense Union force under the command of General George B. McClellan won a battle in Maryland against the South's General Robert E. Lee at Antietam (Sharpsburg). The victory gave Lincoln the green light to issue his proclamation publicly, with a date by which it would go into effect set for January 1, 1863.

As the night of December 31 sped toward midnight, Douglass and several of his fellow abolitionists gathered in a large hall in Boston to celebrate the Emancipation Proclamation. They had all gathered, noted Douglass, in the same spirit, anxious to see slavery receive what they hoped would be its first death throe. Writing in his memoirs, Douglass noted: "We were waiting and listening as for a bolt from the sky . . . we were watching . . . by the dim light of the stars for the dawn of a new day . . . we were longing for the answer to the agonizing prayers

Douglass's Later Years

Following the Civil War, Frederick Douglass continued his public service, even though his lifelong campaign to bring down slavery in the United States had ended. He was appointed president of the Freedman's Savings Bank, a new financial institution for the nation's newly freed blacks. In 1872, his house in Rochester, which had served as his home for many years, burned down, and he moved to Washington, D.C. Arson was suspected. That same year, he became the first black vice presidential nominee, sharing the Equal Rights Party ticket with presidential candidate Victoria Woodhull. The nomination was made without his prior knowledge, but he did not withdraw from the race.

He became marshal of the District of Columbia in 1877, and by the late 1880s, he was chosen as minister resident and consul general to the Republic of Haiti, as well as the charge d'affaires for the Dominican Republic. His wife, Anna, died in 1882. In 1884, he married a white feminist named Helen Pitts. Their interracial marriage soon faced much criticism, including from both her family and his children, who felt he had turned his back on their mother's legacy. Between 1886 and 1887, the couple traveled throughout Europe, with Douglass continuing his longstanding speaking tours.

In 1888, at the Republican National Convention, Douglass was nominated for president during a roll call vote, even though he did not win the nomination. Seven years later, in 1895, while attending a session of the National Council of Women in Washington, Douglass died of a heart attack. He is buried in Mount Hope Cemetery in Rochester, New York.

of centuries." At the stroke of midnight, the gathered crowd shouted and cheered, for slavery appeared on its way to extinction in the United States.

"MEN OF COLOR, TO ARMS!"

The arrival of the New Year put the Emancipation Proclamation into effect, signaling that one day, perhaps soon, slavery would come to an end in the United States. At this time, Douglass stepped up his campaign for blacks to be included in the Federal armed services. The first blacks to be allowed to join the Union military cause were not given guns to engage in combat. They were merely support troops. They were not even paid the same as white soldiers, and they had to wear different uniforms. Douglass pushed constantly for blacks to be given combat opportunities. In a March 2, 1863, article in his abolitionist paper, he wrote an editorial titled, "Men of Color, To Arms!" in which he argued for blacks to demand to be given the opportunity to fight:

> Action! Action! Not criticism, is the plain duty of this hour. . . . The iron gate of our prison stands half open. One gallant rush from the North will fling it wide open, while four millions of our brothers and sisters shall march out into liberty. The chance is now given you to end in a day the bondage of centuries.

The call for blacks to fight did not fall, ultimately, on deaf ears. As the war continued and white casualties mounted by the thousands with each battle, the U.S. Department of War established a Bureau of Colored Troops in May 1863. Massachusetts led the way by creating two black regiments, the 54th and the 55th. Two of Douglass's sons, Lewis and Charles, joined up, along with 185,000 other blacks who would fight for the Union and for the destruction of slavery. The 54th Massachusetts Regiment's most memorable engagement was an unsuccessful, if gallant, charge against Fort Wagner in Charleston.

A MEETING WITH THE PRESIDENT

As the war continued, Douglass kept up his campaigns, pushing for the federal government to bring down slavery. He also fought

One of Douglass's activist duties included recruiting young black men for the Union Army after the Emancipation Proclamation went into effect. When he discovered that the black soldiers received unequal wages to their white counterparts, Douglass addressed this problem by speaking directly with President Abraham Lincoln. Above, a regiment of African-American Union soldiers lines up in 1863.

for black troops to be paid the same as white soldiers. His and other abolitionists' efforts paid off when Congress passed the Thirteenth Amendment to the U.S. Constitution on January 31, 1865, which officially abolished slavery in the United States. But this did not put an end to Douglass's struggle for fellow members of the black race. Slavery might have ended, but this did not mean that blacks, even those who were free, could vote. That spring, near the end of the Civil War, Douglass and other black leaders met with Abraham Lincoln to encourage his support for black suffrage, beginning with black military veterans and those blacks who were educated and literate. Lincoln agreed to do what he could toward those two goals.

But Lincoln was not able to help Douglass and his fellow black leaders accomplish these noble tasks. Within a week of the end of the four-year-long war, an assassin shot Lincoln in a theater in Washington, killing the president. The loss of Lincoln was a blow to Douglass, who mourned that the country, as well as his people, had lost an advocate. As noted by historian Melva Lawson Ware, Douglass would write:

> But, dying as he did die, by the red hand of violence, killed, assassinated, taken off without warning, not because of personal hate—for no man who knew Abraham Lincoln could hate him—but because of his fidelity to union and liberty, he is doubly dear to us, and his memory will be precious forever.

Frederick Douglass attended President Lincoln's memorial service and managed to speak, even though he was not scheduled to deliver any address. A prominent attorney gave a memorial speech for the assassinated president, but some of those in attendance did not feel the address did Lincoln's legacy justice. Douglass, noted for his eloquence, was asked to speak on the spot. With reluctance, he stepped forward and spoke, despite having not prepared any address.

In his speech, he admitted that Lincoln had waited far too long before supporting emancipation for black slaves. He noted that Lincoln, prior to his presidency, had opposed slavery's expansion into the western territories but had not campaigned for slavery's abolition. But Douglass's criticisms of the president were softened by other words of praise for the slain leader. As recalled by historian Henry Louis Gates, Jr., Douglass noted: "Can any colored man, or any white man friendly to the freedom of all men, ever forget the night which followed the first day of January 1863, when the world was to see if Abraham Lincoln would prove to be as good as his word?" Such words inspired those in attendance, who gave Douglass a standing ovation. The story is told that Mary Todd Lincoln, the president's widow, appreciated Douglass's words so much that she gave him the president's favorite walking cane as a gift.

A CHANGED VOICE

With war over, slavery ended, and blacks having been accepted in the military as combat troops, Frederick Douglass had proven himself a true leader, not only of those of his own race, but of the country and its new directions. For decades prior to the war, Douglass had been a constant voice in the wilderness, condemning the institution of slavery with its horrors and destructive nature. Few who fought for its abolition knew slavery from direct experience as well as Frederick Douglass did. Those years of slavery, abuse, and humiliation had managed to give him unique insights into the system of perpetual night for millions of black men and women. His life became a testament to the power of endurance in the face of hatred, and his voice served as a call that would finally bring daylight to night, hope to a downtrodden race, and a new path of freedom for the country's future.

Glossary

ABOLITIONISM   The process of freeing slaves immediately.

BREVET   A temporary advancement in military rank often made in the field without official approval.

CONFEDERATES OR CONFEDERACY   Those who supported secession from the United States and who fought for the South during the Civil War.

CONSCRIPTION   Forced recruitment of enlistees for military service; refers to a draft.

DEMERIT   A negative citation for an infraction of a set of rules.

DEMOCRAT PARTY   The political party formed during the age of Andrew Jackson, which supported the Jackson presidency.

EMANCIPATION PROCLAMATION   Official announcement made by President Abraham Lincoln in the fall of 1862 that "freed" all slaves held in states in rebellion against the United States.

EXECUTOR   A person designated to carry out the stipulations of a will when someone dies.

FLANK   Either end of a line of massed soldiers, signified as an army's "left" or "right."

FREE SOILERS   A political party created during the 1840s and later replaced by the Republican Party. The party did not support the western expansion of slavery.

INDENTURED SERVANT   A poor immigrant to America during the colonial period who could not pay for his or her ship passage, but who worked for someone who had covered the cost of the passage. A typical time frame for an indentured servant was seven years.

KANSAS-NEBRASKA ACT   An 1854 act of Congress that created the territories of Kansas and Nebraska and opened them up to the potential of slavery.

MANIFEST DESTINY   The belief held by many Americans during the first half of the nineteenth century that the United States was "destined" to take control of the western regions, including the Rockies and the Pacific coast.

MILITIA   Usually refers to troops provided on a state level.

POPULAR SOVEREIGNTY   The political theory that encouraged the residents of a western territory to vote whether or not they wanted slavery to exist in their future state.

REAR ECHELON   The support personnel to those serving on the front lines of a military unit.

REBELS   Commonplace term for Southerners who supported the Confederacy during the Civil War.

RECONNAISSANCE   To gather intelligence about an enemy, its strength, and its position.

REGIMENT   A unit of an army made up of several battalions or squadrons of soldiers organized into one large group, usually commanded by a colonel. It is smaller than a brigade.

REPUBLICANS   Those holding membership or identity in the Republican Party, which was formed during the early 1850s and was generally a northern party in its base.

SECEDE   To separate or remove a state from a larger state or country.

STATES' RIGHTS   The political theory that proposes that the rights of the states come first over the power of the federal government.

SUFFRAGE   The right to vote.

TRANSCONTINENTAL RAILROAD   Rail line completed in 1869 that stretched across the continent from the Pacific coast to the Atlantic coast.

UNION   Common reference in the early nineteenth century to the United States.

WHIG PARTY   U.S. political party created during the 1830s in response to President Andrew Jackson. The party opposed many of Jackson's political views and remained in existence for about 20 years, until the early 1850s. The Republican Party established in the early 1850s included former Whigs.

Bibliography

Alexander, Bevin. *Robert E. Lee's Civil War*. Avon, Mass.: Adams Media Corporation, 1998.

Allen, Felicity. *Jefferson Davis: The Unconquerable Heart*. Columbia, Mo.: The University of Missouri Press, 2000.

Basler, Roy P. *Collected Works of Abraham Lincoln*. New Brunswick, N.J.: Rutgers University Press, 1955.

Davis, Jefferson. *The Rise and Fall of the Confederate Government*. 1881. Reprint, New York: Da Capo Press, 1990.

Donald, David Herbert. *Lincoln*. New York: Simon & Schuster, 1995.

Dowdey, Clifford. *Lee*. New York: Bonanza Books, 1965.

Earle, Peter. *Robert E. Lee*. New York: Saturday Review Press, 1973.

Gallagher, Gary W. *The American Civil War: This Mighty Scourge of War*. New York: Osprey Publishing, 2003.

Gates, Henry Louis, ed. and Frederick Douglass. *Douglass' Autobiographies*. New York: Library of America, 1994.

Jackson, Mary Anna. *Memoirs of Stonewall Jackson, by His Widow*. Louisville, Ky: 1895.

Lee, Douglas Southall Freeman. *Lee of Virginia*. New York: Charles Scribner's Sons, 1958.

Lee, Douglas Southall Freeman. *R.E. Lee: A Biography*. New York: Charles Scribner's Sons, 1934.

McFeely, William S. *Grant: A Biography*. New York: W.W. Norton, 1981.

McPherson, James M. *Battle Cry of Freedom*. New York: Oxford University Press, 1988.

Robertson, James I., Jr. *Stonewall Jackson: The Man, the Soldier, the Legend*. New York: MacMillan Publishing, 1997.

Roland, Charles P. *Reflections on Lee: An Assessment*. Mechanicsburg, Pa.: Stackpole Books, 1993.

Smith, Francis H. *History of the Virginia Military Institute*. Richmond, Va.: Evergreen Press, 1988.

Sobel, Brian. "Battlefield Leader: General Robert E. Lee." *Armchair General*, May 2007.

Thomas, Sandra. "Frederick Douglass." Rochester History Resources. Available online. URL: http://www.history.rochester.edu/class/douglass/home.html. Accessed December 9, 2008.

Ward, Geoffrey. *The Civil War: An Illustrated History*. New York: Random House, 1990.

Ware, Melva Lawson. *Frederick Douglass: Freedom's Force*. Alexandria, Va.: Time-Life Books, 1998.

Further Resources

ABRAHAM LINCOLN

Ruffin, Frances. *Abraham Lincoln: From Pioneer to President*. New York: Sterling Publishing, 2007.

Stone, Tanya Lee. *Abraham Lincoln*. New York: DK Publishing, 2004.

JEFFERSON DAVIS

Hale, Sarah Elder. *Jefferson Davis and the Confederacy*. Peterborough, N.H.: Cobblestone, 2005.

Williams, Jean Kinney. *Jefferson Davis: President of the Confederate States*. Mankato, Minn.: Coughlan Publishing, 2005.

ROBERT E. LEE

Anderson, Paul Christopher. *Robert E. Lee: Legendary Commander of the Confederacy*. New York: Rosen Publishing Group, 2001.

Bradford, Gamaliel. *Lee the American*. San Diego: Dover Publications, 2004.

Gillis, Jennifer Blizin. *Robert E. Lee: Confederate Commander*. Mankato, Minn.: Coughlan Publishing, 2005.

Grabowski, Patricia A. *Robert E. Lee: Confederate General*. Broomall, Pa.: Chelsea House Publishers, 2000.

Ransom, Candice F. *Robert E. Lee*. Minneapolis: Lerner Publishing Group, 2006.

ULYSSES S. GRANT

Gregson, Susan R. *Ulysses S. Grant*. Mankato, Minn.: Coughlan Publishing, 2000.

McLeese, Don. *Ulysses S. Grant*. Shippensburg, Pa.: Rourke Publishing, 2005.

Riehecky, Janet. *Ulysses S. Grant*. New York: Children's Press, 2004.

THOMAS "STONEWALL" JACKSON

Doak, Robin Santos. *Thomas Stonewall Jackson: Confederate General*. Mankato, Minn.: Coughlan Publishing, 2005.

McLeese, Don. *Stonewall Jackson*. Shippensburg, Pa.: Rourke Publishing, 2005.

FREDERICK DOUGLASS

Burchard, Peter. *Frederick Douglass: For the Great Family of Man*. New York: Simon & Schuster Children's Publishing, 2007.

Davidson, Margaret. *Frederick Douglass Fights for Freedom*. New York: Scholastic, 1988.

Mayer, Cassie. *Frederick Douglass*. Portsmouth, N.H.: Heinemann, 2007.

WEB SITES

Arlington House: The Robert E. Lee Memorial
http://www.nps.gov/arho

Beauvoir: The Jefferson Davis Home and Presidential Library
http://www.beauvoir.org

Fredericksburg and Spotsylvania County Battlefields Memorial
http://www.nps.gov/frsp/js.htm

The Lincoln Institute Presents: Abraham Lincoln's Classroom
http://www.abrahamlincolnsclassroom.org

National Park Service: Douglass' Life
http://www.nps.gov/archive/frdo/fdlife.htm

PBS: Africans in America. Frederick Douglass
http://www.pbs.org/wgbh/aia/part4/4p1539.html

Rochester University History Resources: A Biography of the Life of Frederick Douglass
http://www.history.rochester.edu/class/douglass/home.html

The White House: Biography of Abraham Lincoln
http://www.whitehouse.gov/history/presidents/al16.html

The White House: Biography of Ulysses S. Grant
http://www.whitehouse.gov/history/presidents/ug18.html

Picture Credits

PAGE

18: ©Morton Beebe/CORBIS

22: © Hulton Archive/Getty Images

26: Alexander Hesler/AP Images

35: Courtesy of the Library of Congress, LC-USZ62-90

42: AP Images

47: AP Images

55: ©Bettmann/CORBIS

60: Courtesy of the Library of Congress, LC-USZ62-92039

67: AP Images

73: © National Portrait Gallery, Smithsonian Institution/Art Resource, NY

82: James A. Finley/ AP Images

88: Courtesy of the Library of Congress, LC-USZ62-132504

93: © Hulton Archive/Getty Images

103: Courtesy of the Library of Congress, LC-USZ62-132551

108: © Hulton Archive/Getty Images

114: © Snark/Art Resource, NY

120: AP Images

130: © Hulton Archive/Getty Images

Index

About
the Authors

TIM MCNEESE is associate professor of history at York College in York, Nebraska, where he is in his seventeenth year of college instruction. Professor McNeese earned an associate of arts degree from York College, a bachelor of arts in history and political science from Harding University, and a master of arts in history from Missouri State University. A prolific author of books for elementary school, middle school, high school, and college readers, McNeese has published more than 100 books and educational materials over the past 20 years, on everything from the founding of early New York to Hispanic authors. His writing has earned him a citation in the library reference work *Contemporary Authors* and multiple citations in *Best Books for Young Teen Readers*. In 2006, McNeese appeared on the History Channel program *Risk Takers, History Makers: John Wesley Powell and the Grand Canyon*. He was a faculty member at the 2006 Tony Hillerman Writers Conference in Albuquerque. His wife, Beverly, is an assistant professor of English at York College. They have two married children, Noah and Summer, and three grandchildren, Ethan, Adrianna, and Finn William. Tim and Bev McNeese sponsored study trips for college students on the Lewis and Clark Trail in 2003 and 2005 and to the American Southwest in 2008. You may contact Professor McNeese at tdmcneese@york.edu.